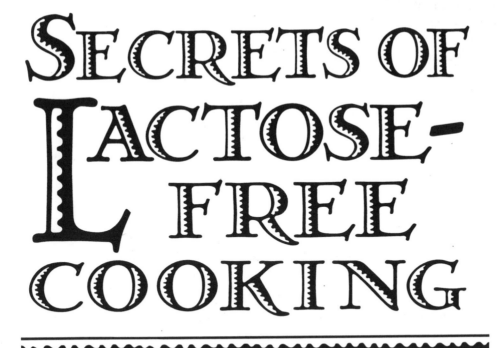

SECRETS OF LACTOSE-FREE COOKING

Over 150 delicious dairy-free and lactose-reduced recipes – from breakfast to dinner

ARLENE BURLANT, RD

Avery Publishing Group

Garden City Park, New York

Text illustrator: John Wincek
Cover photograph: Amy Reichman
Cover designer: William Gonzalez
In-house editor: Elaine Will Sparber
Typesetter: Bonnie Freid
Printer: Paragon Press, Honesdale, PA

Library of Congress Cataloging-in-Publication Data

Burlant, Arlene.
    Secrets of lactose-free cooking: over 150 delicious dairy-free and
lactose-reduced recipes—from breakfast to dinner / by Arlene
Burlant.
        p.   cm.
    Includes bibliographical references and index.
    ISBN 0-89529-724-8
    1. Milk-free diet—Recipes.   2. Lactose intolerance—Diet
therapy—Recipes.   I. Title.
RM234.5.B875 1996
641.5'63—dc20   95-50595
                                                 CIP

Printed in the United States of America.

10   9   8   7   6   5   4   3   2

Contents

To Anita and Morris,
without whose dietary problems
this book would not have been written.

Acknowledgments

It is a pleasure to thank the many sources and suppliers of the foods highlighted in this book for their cooperation in furnishing dietary information as well as their expansive discussions about lactose sensitivity. It is satisfying, indeed, to know of such continuing interest in this subject.

This book would not have materialized without the encouragement of Rudy Shur, Karen Hay, Joanne Abrams, and Elaine Will Sparber of Avery Publishing Group. Their support and outstanding professional judgment transformed my collection of recipes into a useful and attractive reference volume.

Many people tested the recipes described herein, and to them I am most grateful. But I give special thanks to my husband, Bill, who felt obligated to check, with enthusiasm, and on a continuing basis, the dessert section to ensure that those recipes met my high standards.

Preface

It is ironic that milk—the near-perfect food—is not easily tolerated by perhaps as much as three-quarters of the adult population. However, a good deal is known medically about this troublesome condition. As a dietitian, with access to the latest nutritional and clinical findings, I therefore set about several years ago to devise tasty, wholesome dishes prepared without dairy products, or with reduced lactose products, that would alleviate or eliminate uncomfortable reactions in persons sensitive to milk products.

Over the years, I have collected a number of recipes that members of my family as well as my patients have found useful. I have re-created beef Stroganoff, "cream" soups, breads, cakes, and ice creams, among other favorites, to meet the needs of individuals sensitive to lactose. I also dipped into the vast resource of ethnic cooking—many cultures use little or no milk products—to add variety to this collection.

Since it is important that our eating habits conform, where possible, to the recommendations of the Surgeon General's Report, I have included the relevant nutrient values, plus the diabetic exchanges, for each recipe. A glance at this dietary information before preparing a recipe will assist you in menu planning.

I am sure you will discover that dairy-free and reduced-lactose dishes can be tasty and flavorful, while still contributing, in an important way, to a nutritious diet.

Introduction

One of the most important nutrients in milk is the natural sugar lactose. Lactose is a complex substance made up of two simpler sugars—glucose and galactose. In the human body, lactose may play a role in promoting the metabolism of fat, protein, and minerals such as calcium, magnesium, and manganese.

Although lactose occurs only in milk, this unique sugar finds its way into a great variety of common foods, including breads, cakes, cereals, cooking mixes, prepared meats and fish, and soups. Less commonly, it is found in items such as prepared horseradish and sausage. It may even be found in the formulas of some drug tablets and capsules.

To digest lactose, the human body normally produces an enzyme called lactase. The function of this enzyme is to break down lactose into its simpler and readily digested building blocks. When the body does not manufacture lactase in sufficient quantity, it cannot digest the milk sugar. The undigested lactose then ferments in the small intestine. People who are lactase deficient, or lactose intolerant, may exhibit symptoms such as gas, bloating, cramps, or diarrhea when they ingest dairy products.

Certain nondairy foods—including peas, lima beans, beets, liver, sweetbreads, and brains—contain glycosides, which are large, complex molecules that occur in nature. Glycosides can be metabolized to lactose, and individuals sensitive to lactose may also need to avoid foods containing glycosides.

About three-quarters of all adults exhibit the most common type of lactose intolerance: primary adult lactase deficiency. In the United States alone, at least 30 million adults are affected. Nor is lactose intolerance uncommon among children. For example, many Greek and Israeli children are lactose sensitive by age five, with about 80 percent exhibiting the condition by age twelve. In China, Jamaica, Bangladesh, and Peru, 80 percent of all youngsters are lactose sensitive by age three. But some encouraging recent patient studies show that many individuals who experience discomfort due to lactose sensitivity, can still drink as much as one glass of whole milk every day with no significant problems. It seems that there are degrees of lactose intolerance. While some people can tolerate no dairy products at all, others can enjoy a limited amount without discomfort. In other cases, people who are not lactose intolerant may experience some of the symptoms simply because they *perceive* themselves as being lactose sensitive.

While the inability to break down lactose increases

with age, the digestive system develops alternate mechanisms to metabolize milk sugar. The good news is that lactose intolerance is not a disease. In fact, since our ancestors did not drink milk past early childhood, and therefore had no need for the enzyme lactase, it may be that the normal human genetic path leads to low lactase, and that those who possess the enzyme and can tolerate dairy products represent the abnormal population.

Some lactose intolerance may also occur due to a recurrent intestinal problem such as an intestinal infection, as a result of gastric surgery, as a result of a deficiency of another enzyme, with use of a medication such as an antibiotic or anti-inflammatory drug, or as a result of exposure to therapeutic doses of high-energy radiation. In these cases, the lactose sensitivity may disappear after the treatment or medication is discontinued. And there exists a very rare genetically derived lactose sensitivity in newborns that must be treated at birth.

A less common problem with dairy products—and one not related to lactase deficiency—is an allergic reaction to the protein in cow's milk. This sensitivity is exhibited by a small fraction of infants. While such an allergy may give rise to gastrointestinal distress, it usually is accompanied by wheezing, rash, and runny nose. For infants allergic to cow's milk, formulas based on protein from soybeans are available. For infants allergic to both soybean and cow's-milk protein, special preparations made from predigested milk protein can be used. Fortunately, immune-derived allergies such as these usually disappear before the age of three.

It is important for all people to consult health-care professionals for information and advice on health and dietary matters. Doing this is especially important for lactose-intolerant individuals because in a small number of cases, an underlying intestinal disease may accompany the lactose problem. And, as already mentioned, some people may just *believe* that they have a lactose sensitivity, giving rise to some of the symptoms.

REDUCED-LACTOSE MILK AND MILK PRODUCTS

Most lactose-intolerant individuals adjust their diets by restricting their use of milk products, that is, by limiting their intake of milk, cheese, and ice cream. However,

eliminating lactose-containing foods such as milk and cheese can generate other problems, since these foods are important sources of nutrients such as calcium, vitamins A and D, and the vitamin B group.

Before you reduce your intake of these critical foods, you should consider the following:

- Consuming milk in small servings (four ounces or less) distributed throughout the day has been found to reduce or eliminate discomfort due to lactose intolerance.

- Consuming milk with solid food has been found to reduce or eliminate discomfort due to lactose intolerance.

- Whole milk is often tolerated better than low-fat milk.

- Cocoa and chocolate milk are often tolerated better than unflavored milk.

- Most aged cheeses, such as Swiss and Cheddar, are often tolerated better than other cheeses because of their low lactose contents.

In addition, some studies suggest that a gradual increase in the consumption of lactose-containing foods may result in lessened lactose sensitivity.

Reduced-lactose and lactose-free milk, such as Dairy Ease and Lactaid, are available, and may be tolerated better than untreated milk. These products contain the enzyme lactase, which converts the lactose into glucose and galactose, two sugars that do not cause discomfort. But the free glucose formed may introduce problems for special groups, including some diabetics and infants sensitive to sugars other than lactose. Reduced-lactose milk can be used in place of unmodified milk in virtually all recipes. Low-lactose skim milk is also available. The tolerance to cultured buttermilk and sweet acidophilus milk is similar to that for whole milk.

Yogurt is often well tolerated by milk-sensitive individuals because yogurt cultures produce the needed enzyme lactase. However, since pasteurization inactivates the enzyme, nonpasteurized yogurt is often better tolerated. Nonpasteurized yogurts are made by Dannon, Columbo, Yoplait, Kraft, and Breyers. A cheese substitute useful in some recipes can be created by filtering the solids from most of these yogurts using a fine strainer developed for this purpose. (For directions on how to make yogurt cheese, see page 155.)

Reduced-lactose cottage cheese is available from Friendship and Lactaid, and low-lactose American cheese is offered by Lactaid. Many other companies also offer reduced-lactose cheeses.

Ice cream containing 70 percent less lactose than the conventional product is available from Edy's.

USING LACTOSE-FREE FOODS

The incorporation of dairy substitute products into the diet often is a good way to deal with lactose sensitivity. An impressive variety of dairy substitute items is available, and more products are being introduced every year. Check your local food stores for the items available in your area.

The following list offers a few examples of the more popular substitute dairy items currently found in supermarkets and health food stores:

- **Tofu**, made from soybeans, is a digestible protein-complete food that is available in a variety of forms and textures. An eight-ounce serving provides a substantial percentage of an adult's daily protein and calcium requirements.

- **Soymilk**, derived from soybeans, is nutritionally quite complete, supplying many of the important nutrients present in milk but without milk's lactose. Soymilk is available from many sources, including Eden Foods, Worthington Foods, and Loma Linda Foods. Low-fat and nonfat soymilks are also available, as is soymilk fortified with vitamins and minerals.

- **Milk substitutes** from sources other than soy are also available. Wholesome and Hearty makes Almondmylk, a beverage derived from rice syrup and almonds, while Imagine Foods produces Rice Dream, a rice-based nondairy beverage.

- **Cream and whipping cream substitutes** are made from lactose-free vegetable oils, such as soy oil. Popular whipping "creams" are Hunt's Reddi-Whip, Rich's Rich Whip, Whitehouse's Presto Whip, and Cool Whip. Cream substitutes include Rich's Coffee Rich and Poly Rich, and Carnation's Coffee-Mate. A *nondairy sour cream* called Soymage is made by Soyco.

- **Milk-free margarine**, made from vegetable oil, is offered by Imperial, Mazola, Manischewitz, Mar-Parv, Mother's, Fleischmann's, Weight Watchers, and Heart Beat, among others.

- **Nondairy cheeses**, made from vegetable oil or other foods, such as tofu; and *lactose-free cheeses*, made from lactose-free milk, are available from many sources. Formagg makes mozzarella, provolone, ricotta, cream, Cheddar, and Parmesan cheeses. Che Soya produces Cheddar and Swiss cheeses. Mrs. Margareten offers mozzarella, Parmesan, Swiss, cream, and Monterey jack cheeses. Soya-Kass sells tofu-based cream cheese. Toffuti makes nondairy cream cheese. Parvcheezy, Heart Beat, and Tofu Rella all market Cheddar cheeses. And Soyco specializes in Parmesan cheese.

- **Nondairy yogurt**, based on soybeans, is available from White Wave, Inc.

- **Lactose-free ice creams** are made from lactose-free vegetable oils, such as soy oil. Some popular brands are Tofulite, made by Loft; Tofutti, made by Tofu-Time; and Ice Bean, made by Farm Foods.

- **Lactose-free sorbets**, made from fruits and sugar, are produced by Sharon's, Häagen-Dazs, Friuli, and Cyrk.

Many other lactose-free foods can be found in food stores and health food stores. For example, Ener-G-Foods offers a variety of lactose-free breads, including rice, tapioca, potato, poi, and papas breads; muffins and scones; cakes, cookies, and doughnuts; baking mixes; waffles; and beverages.

Often, a dairy substitute product cannot be used simply as a straight replacement for the milk-containing item. Many whipping-cream substitutes cannot be sufficiently whipped, milk-free margarine often browns when heated excessively, and tofu becomes rubbery when overcooked. Nondairy cheeses do not always taste exactly like their natural counterparts, often exhibit quite a different texture, and usually are best added at the end of the recipe, after the other ingredients have been cooked. Soy-based milk sometimes gives an unwanted color to the final dish and cannot be heated to a high temperature. Furthermore, since the different brands of soymilk are formulated with different kinds and concentrations of ingredients (such as flavorings and sweeteners), each brand responds differently in recipes. When you substitute soymilk for cream, you may need to add vegetable oil to the soymilk. Even reduced-lactose products need to be used with caution. For example, enzyme-treated cow's milk, such as milk with Lactaid added, is sweeter than unmodified milk, so that less sweetener is needed when using the milk in a recipe. For all of these reasons and more, you should plan on several test runs when developing a new recipe to get the new dish to meet your taste and texture requirements.

As with all foods, read labels carefully before purchasing dairy substitute products. Many of these products contain significant amounts of sugar, and many contain saturated fats. Choose brands that are enriched with important nutrients and that contain the least amounts of saturated oils such as coconut, palm, or palm kernel—the so-called tropical oils.

EATING A BALANCED DIET

When maintaining a lactose-reduced or lactose-free diet, you must ensure that you replace an adequate amount of the nutrients lost as a result of your reduced intake of milk and milk products.

Calcium, abundant in milk, is one of the most important elements for the proper growth and functioning of the human body. Table 1 presents the daily allowances for calcium recommended by the National Institutes of Health.

Calcium, however, is not the only important nutrient that milk (both whole and skim) furnishes. Two cups of milk supplies 40 percent of the daily requirement of protein, 20 percent of the daily requirement of vitamin A, 50 percent of vitamin D, 50 percent of vitamin B2 (riboflavin), and 60 percent of vitamin B12. These nutrients occur in the same amounts in both untreated and enzyme-treated milks. For truly nondairy diets, other sources of these dietary essentials

Table 1. Daily Calcium Requirements

	Age	Calcium
Infants	birth to 6 months	400 mg
	6 months to 1 year	600 mg
Children	1 to 10 years	800 mg
Adolescents	11 to 18 years	1,200 mg
Adults	19 years and over	1,200 mg
Pregnant, breast-feeding, or post-menopausal women		1,200–1,600 mg

are needed to ensure an adequate supply. Some additional sources are:

- **Calcium**—leafy green vegetables, such as kale and collards; canned salmon and sardines (with bones); almonds; citrus fruits.
- **Protein**—poultry; meat; fish; soy products; pasta or bread in combination with beans.
- **Vitamin A**—liver; dark green leafy vegetables; carrots; sweet potatoes; apricots.
- **Vitamin D**—liver; eggs; fish liver oils.
- **Vitamin B2**—liver; dark green leafy vegetables; whole grain foods.
- **Vitamin B12**—liver; fish; eggs.

Table 2 shows the nutrient content of some common nondairy foods important in lactose-free and lactose-reduced diets.

The recipes in this book conform as much as possible to the dietary guidelines set forth by the Surgeon General's "Report on Nutrition and Health," aimed at reducing, in some measure, the risks of heart attack, stroke, and cancer. These guidelines include reducing saturated and total fat (for example, by using puréed vegetables instead of heavy cream to thicken soups), using fish in place of meat, using more high-fiber foods, reducing egg yolks and egg-yolk products (for example, by using egg whites, egg substitutes, and egg-free mayonnaise dressing), using less organ meats, and using more complex carbohydrates (breads, pasta, and vegetables).

Table 2. Approximate Percentage of Adult Daily Requirements of Nutrients in Selected Nondairy Foods

Product	Calcium	Protein	Vitamin A	Vitamin D	Vitamin B_2	Vitamin B_{12}
Almonds, 1 ounce	10%	9%	0	0	12%	0
Bread, wheat, 2 slices	6%	7%	0	0	11%	37%
Carrots, ½ cup, raw	3%	Some	400%	0	3%	0
Chicken, white skinless meat, 3 ounces, broiled	Some	40%	Some	0	6%	566%
Egg, 1 large, cooked	4%	13%	7%	7%	12%	12%
Egg substitute, 1½ ounces	3%	12%	25%	Some	11%	Some
Haddock, 3 ounces, broiled	4%	40%	Some	0	3%	20%
Liver, 3 ounces, broiled	Some	40%	800%	9%	270%	1,200%
Salmon, canned, 3 ounces[1]	25%	40%	Some	Some	6%	80%
Sardines, canned, 3 ounces[1]	25%	40%	Some	Some	6%	70%
Soymilk, 6 ounces[2]	Some	9%	Some	0	8%	0
Spinach, ½ cup, cooked[3]	17%	8%	150%	0	6%	11%
Tofu, 4 ounces	20%	30%	4%	0	6%	0

[1] With bones.

[2] These values are for a particular soy product from one manufacturer; products from other sources may yield different values.

[3] Not all the calcium in spinach may be absorbed by the body. Other green vegetables high in calcium and vitamin A are collards, kale, beet greens, turnip greens, and broccoli.

According to the most recent U.S. Department of Agriculture recommendations, the average adult's daily diet should include six to eleven servings of bread, cereal, rice, and pasta; two to five servings each of fruits and vegetables; two to three servings of milk and cheese; two to three servings of meat, fish, eggs, beans, and nuts; and only very small servings of fats, oils, and sweets.

TIPS FOR USING LACTOSE-MODIFIED RECIPES

The recipes collected in this book are based both on lactose-free products and on those foods generally tolerated by lactose-sensitive individuals.

Some ethnic groups use little or no milk in cooking, and are therefore good sources of lactose-free meals, as well as of ideas for new dishes. For example, Chinese and Japanese meat dishes as well as Indian recipes are virtually milk-free (but watch out for Indian dishes calling for milk curd). Jewish kosher-labeled meat-containing and parve

foods contain no dairy products. And many Spanish dishes are milk-free. Of course, reduced-lactose milk may be substituted for unmodified milk in almost any dish.

For this cookbook, I employ several strategies to reduce or eliminate lactose from the diet. In a number of recipes that normally use dairy products, I instead use dairy substitutes or reduced-lactose products. For example, in place of milk, I suggest using water, fruit juice, soymilk, nondairy cream diluted with water, or reduced-lactose whole, low-fat, or skim milk. In place of dairy products added to give foods a creamlike consistency, I suggest using common thickeners based on starch, flour, or puréed vegetables or fruits. Some recipes I reformulated to completely eliminate both dairy products and their substitutes. For convenience and completeness, and where a desirable nutrient is present, I have also included in this book some popular recipes that are normally lactose-free.

Reducing or eliminating lactose from the diet does not mean that you can ignore how much salt and fat you consume. The recipes in this collection use, to a large extent, products considered healthy across the board. To reduce cholesterol, plain egg whites or egg white-based egg substitutes are often used in place of whole eggs. (Egg Beaters and Egg Replacer are only two examples of such products.) Low-fat cheeses, mayonnaise, yogurt, and meats are used whenever possible. When a recipe calls for sautéing, a nonstick skillet and/or nonstick cooking spray is recommended. Salt has been omitted as often as feasible, with the understanding that it can be added as desired. Low-sodium meat and chicken bouillon are used whenever possible.

To help you better plan your daily menus, every recipe in this book ends with nutrient and diabetic-exchange information. In the section on nutrient content, the percentage in parentheses represents the percentage of the calories derived from fat. Doctors currently recommend that not more than 30 percent of overall *daily* caloric intake come from fat. Regarding the diabetic-exchange information, the exchanges for your particular situation—especially if the recipe

includes sugar, molasses, or honey—should be discussed with a health professional. Most of the meat exchanges in the recipes are based on very lean meat, for which 7 grams of protein and either 0 or 1 gram of fat equal 1 very lean meat exchange. When oil is a recipe ingredient, use a monounsaturated oil such as canola, olive, or peanut. Additional foods mentioned as part of any serving suggestion or variation as well as optional foods mentioned as part of the recipe are not incorporated in the nutrient or exchange values.

For consistent results, measure all ingredients carefully. The handy Table of Measurements found on page 7 was designed to make accurate measuring a snap, even when halving or doubling recipe amounts.

You will discover as you use this book that lactose-free cooking offers varied, delicious, and healthful dishes. I hope you use the recipes and suggestions offered herein as a foundation upon which you build a more complete repertory of reduced-lactose and lactose-free dishes.

Table of Measurements

VOLUME MEASUREMENT EQUIVALENTS

Pinch or dash	= less than $\frac{1}{8}$ teaspoon			
1 teaspoon	= $\frac{1}{3}$ tablespoon			= $\frac{1}{6}$ fluid ounce
1 tablespoon	= 3 teaspoons			= $\frac{1}{2}$ fluid ounce
2 tablespoons	= $\frac{1}{8}$ cup	= $\frac{1}{16}$ pint		= 1 fluid ounce
4 tablespoons	= $\frac{1}{4}$ cup			= 2 fluid ounces
8 tablespoons	= $\frac{1}{2}$ cup			= 4 fluid ounces
12 tablespoons	= $\frac{3}{4}$ cup			= 6 fluid ounces
16 tablespoons	= 1 cup	= $\frac{1}{2}$ pint		= 8 fluid ounces
$\frac{1}{8}$ cup	= 2 tablespoons			= 1 fluid ounce
$\frac{1}{4}$ cup	= 4 tablespoons			= 2 fluid ounces
$\frac{1}{2}$ cup	= 8 tablespoons			= 4 fluid ounces
$\frac{3}{4}$ cup	= 12 tablespoons	= 6 fluid ounces		
1 cup	= 16 tablespoons	= $\frac{1}{2}$ pint		= 8 fluid ounces
2 cups	= 1 pint	= $\frac{1}{2}$ quart		= 16 fluid ounces
4 cups	= 2 pints	= 1 quart		= 32 fluid ounces
8 cups	= 4 pints	= 2 quarts		= 64 fluid ounces
16 cups	= 8 pints	= 4 quarts	= 1 gallon	= 128 fluid ounces
$\frac{1}{2}$ pint	= 1 cup			= 8 fluid ounces
1 pint	= 2 cups			= 16 fluid ounces
2 pints	= 4 cups	= 1 quart		= 32 fluid ounces
4 pints	= 8 cups	= 2 quarts		= 64 fluid ounces
8 pints	= 16 cups	= 4 quarts	= 1 gallon	= 128 fluid ounces
$\frac{1}{2}$ quart	= 2 cups	= 1 pint		= 16 fluid ounces
1 quart	= 4 cups	= 2 pints		= 32 fluid ounces

WEIGHT MEASUREMENT EQUIVALENTS

1 gram	= 0.04 ounce	
100 grams	= 3.57 ounces	
1 ounce		= 28.35 grams
$\frac{1}{2}$ pound	= 8 ounces	= 226.8 grams
1 pound	= 16 ounces	= 453.6 grams

1

Pancakes, Crêpes, and French Toast

Pancakes and crêpes are delicious served alone, and make balanced, tasty dishes when combined with fish, meat, fruit, or vegetables. They offer the good taste and nutrition of eggs and grain, and can serve both as special Sunday breakfasts or brunches and as the base for more substantial main dishes.

Pancakes

Yield: 4 servings
Prep. time: 15 minutes

1 cup nondairy pancake mix

1 cup soymilk

¼ cup egg substitute

1 tablespoon oil

A breakfast treat especially delicious with nuts or nondairy chocolate chips added to the batter before cooking.

1. In a medium bowl, combine all the ingredients. Stir until no large lumps remain.

2. Lightly coat a griddle with nonstick cooking spray and heat over medium heat. Carefully pour ¼ cup of batter onto the griddle and cook until the underside of the pancake is golden brown and bubbles are popping on the topside, about 1 minute. Gently turn the pancake using a spatula and cook an additional minute. Slide the pancake off the griddle and onto a plate; cover to keep warm. Repeat with the remaining batter.

3. Serve the pancakes hot topped with syrup, compote, fruit, nuts, or nondairy chocolate syrup.

NUTRITIONAL FACTS PER SERVING (2 PANCAKES)

Calories: 167	Protein: 7.5 g	Carbohydrates: 24 g
Calcium: 32 mg	Total Fat: 5 g (27% fat cals)	Saturated Fat: 0.8 g

EXCHANGES, PER SERVING (2 PANCAKES): 1½ Starch; 1 Fat.

Variations

Add ¼ cup blueberries, raspberries, mashed banana, nuts, or nondairy chocolate chips to the batter before cooking.

Apple Pancakes

One of my favorites for Sunday breakfast—a different way to make an outstanding pancake.

Yield: 4 servings
Prep. time: 20 minutes

1. In a small bowl, combine the sugar and cinnamon.

2. Lightly coat a large skillet with nonstick cooking spray. Add the oil, and heat the skillet over medium heat until hot but not smoking. Add the apple slices and sauté until soft. Add the cinnamon sugar and stir. Add the Pancakes batter, being careful to distribute it evenly.

3. Cook the pancake until the underside is golden brown and bubbles are popping on the topside, about 5 minutes. Gently turn the pancake using a spatula and/or fork and cook an additional 2 minutes.

4. Slide the pancake out of the skillet and onto a plate. Cut into quarters and serve immediately.

2 tablespoons sugar

1 teaspoon cinnamon

1 tablespoon oil

1 medium Granny Smith apple, peeled and thinly sliced

1 recipe Pancakes (see page 10), prepared through step 1 only

---

NUTRITIONAL FACTS PER SERVING (¼ PANCAKE)

Calories: 230   Protein: 7.5 g   Carbohydrates: 34 g
Calcium: 36 mg   Total Fat: 7 g (27% fat cals)   Saturated Fat: 0.5 g

---

EXCHANGES, PER SERVING (¼ PANCAKE): 2 Starch; 1½ Fat.

Buckwheat Pancakes

Yield: 8 servings
Prep. time: 20 minutes
plus rising

1 package active dry yeast

2 cups buckwheat flour

½ cup cornmeal

1 tablespoon brown sugar

2½ cups hot water

1 teaspoon baking soda

2 tablespoons oil

1 teaspoon warm water

A great "from scratch" pancake. It takes a bit longer but it is an outstanding recipe.

1. In a large bowl, combine the yeast, buckwheat flour, cornmeal, and brown sugar. Add the hot water and beat with an electric mixer at medium speed for 2 minutes. Cover the bowl loosely with a clean towel and let the batter rise in a warm (about 75°F) place overnight.

2. In the morning, stir the batter well. In a small bowl, combine the baking soda with the oil and warm water; stir until the baking soda is dissolved. Add the baking soda mixture to the batter and mix gently with a fork.

3. Lightly coat a griddle with nonstick cooking spray and heat over medium heat. Carefully pour about 2 tablespoons of batter onto the griddle and cook until the underside of the pancake is golden brown and bubbles are popping on the topside, about 1 minute. Gently turn the pancake using a spatula and cook an additional minute. Slide the pancake off the griddle and onto a plate; cover to keep warm. Repeat with the remaining batter.

4. Serve the pancakes hot with butter and syrup.

NUTRITIONAL FACTS PER SERVING (2 PANCAKES)

Calories: 137	Protein: 3 g	Carbohydrates: 21 g
Calcium: 8 mg	Total Fat: 4 g (26% fat cals)	Saturated Fat: 0.4 g

EXCHANGES, PER SERVING (2 PANCAKES): 1 Starch; 1 Fat.

Crêpes

An attractive, versatile entrée for any meal. Serve them for breakfast filled with fruit or for brunch filled with creamed chicken.

Yield: 6 servings
Prep. time: 20 minutes

1. In a large bowl, combine the eggs with $\frac{1}{2}$ cup of the water; beat well. Add the flour and remaining water, and beat until thoroughly mixed.

2. Lightly coat a 5-inch crêpe pan or heavy skillet with nonstick cooking spray, and place over low heat until hot. Carefully pour 2 tablespoons of batter into the hot pan and tip the pan from side to side to spread the batter over the entire bottom. Cook until the crêpe is set, about 2 to 3 minutes. Gently turn the crêpe using a fork and cook for an additional minute. Slide the crêpe out of the pan and onto a plate or piece of paper towel; cover to keep warm. Repeat with the remaining batter.

3. Serve the crêpes filled with chopped vegetables, fruit, creamed chicken, creamed beef, or shrimp.

3 eggs

$1\frac{1}{2}$ cups water

$1\frac{1}{2}$ cups all-purpose flour

NUTRITIONAL FACTS PER SERVING (3 UNFILLED CRÊPES)

Calories: 140	Protein: 6 g	Carbohydrates: 22 g
Calcium: 19 mg	Total Fat: 3 g (19% fat cals)	Saturated Fat: 1 g

EXCHANGES, PER SERVING (3 UNFILLED CRÊPES): $1\frac{1}{2}$ Starch; $\frac{1}{2}$ Fat.

French Toast

Yield: 4 servings
Prep. time: 10 minutes

Especially good topped with banana slices that have been heated in maple syrup. My children also loved this French toast made in a waffle iron instead of on a griddle.

1 egg

2 tablespoons egg substitute

$\frac{1}{2}$ cup reduced-fat soymilk

$\frac{1}{2}$ teaspoon vanilla extract

4 slices (about 1 inch thick) day-old dairy-free challah, trimmed of crust

Cinnamon to taste

1. In a medium bowl, combine the egg with the egg substitute; mix thoroughly with a fork. Add the soymilk and vanilla extract, and beat well.

2. Lightly coat a griddle with nonstick cooking spray and heat over medium heat.

3. Dip a piece of challah in the egg mixture for 2 to 3 seconds, turning it over to coat both sides. Place it on the griddle and cook until the underside is golden brown. Gently turn the challah using a fork and cook until the other side is golden brown. Remove the toast from the griddle and place on a plate; cover to keep warm.

4. Sprinkle the toast with cinnamon and serve warm.

NUTRITIONAL FACTS PER SERVING (1 SLICE)

Calories: 145	Protein: 5 g	Carbohydrates: 15 g
Calcium: 50 mg	Total Fat: 4.8 g (36% fat cals)	Saturated Fat: 1 g

---

EXCHANGES, PER SERVING (1 SLICE): 1 Starch; 1 Fat.

Baked French Toast

A different way to prepare an all-time favorite.

Yield: 8 servings
Prep. time: 10 minutes
Baking time: 20–30 minutes

1. Preheat the oven to 350°F.

2. Line the bottom of a 13-x-9-inch baking dish with the challah.

3. In a blender, combine the eggs, egg whites, honey, water, vanilla extract, and lemon rind. Leaving the blender running, add the tofu cubes 1 by 1. Purée until the mixture is smooth, then pour the mixture into the baking dish over the bread. Sprinkle lightly with the nutmeg.

4. Place the baking dish in the oven and bake until the custard has set, about 20 to 30 minutes.

5. Remove the toast from the oven and serve plain or with fresh fruit.

8 slices (about 1 inch thick) day-old dairy-free challah, trimmed of crust

3 eggs

3 egg whites

¼ cup honey

¼ cup water

1 teaspoon vanilla extract

1 teaspoon grated lemon rind

1 pound soft tofu, drained and cut into 1-inch cubes

½ teaspoon ground nutmeg, as garnish

NUTRITIONAL FACTS PER SERVING (1 SLICE)

Calories: 180	Protein: 4.6 g	Carbohydrates: 28 g
Calcium: 51 mg	Total Fat: 5 g (25% fat cals)	Saturated Fat: 1 g

EXCHANGES, PER SERVING (1 SLICE): 2 Starch; 1 Fat.

Lactose Intolerance
Versus Milk Protein Allergy

An allergic reaction to the protein present in milk is very different from lactose intolerance, which is the inability to digest the milk sugar lactose. An allergy to milk occurs most often in infants, who outgrow the sensitivity by age three. Like all allergies, this is an immunological response, and usually manifests itself as wheezing, rash, runny nose, and gastrointestinal distress. In such cases, there is often a family history of food allergy. On the other hand, the incidence of lactose intolerance increases with age, and manifests itself as gas, bloating, cramps, or diarrhea.

Waffles

Yield: 6 servings
Prep. time: 20 minutes

1¾ cups all-purpose flour

3 teaspoons baking powder

⅛ teaspoon cinnamon

2 eggs

2 egg whites

¾ cup water

½ cup mashed soft tofu

2 tablespoons vanilla extract

1 tablespoon honey

1 tablespoon nondairy
   margarine, melted

A "from scratch" recipe, but worth the effort.

1. Preheat the waffle iron. (The waffle iron used in this recipe makes 3 waffles.)

2. In a large bowl, combine the flour, baking powder, and cinnamon. In a separate bowl, combine the eggs and egg whites; mix thoroughly with a fork. To the eggs, add the water, tofu, vanilla extract, honey, and margarine; mix until smooth. Add the liquid ingredients to the dry ingredients and stir just until the dry ingredients are moistened.

3. Pour about half the batter into the waffle iron and bake until the steaming stops and the waffle is golden brown. Remove the waffle from the iron and place on a plate; cover to keep warm. Repeat with the remaining batter.

4. Serve the waffles hot.

NUTRITIONAL FACTS PER SERVING (1 WAFFLE)

Calories: 208	Protein: 7 g	Carbohydrates: 34 g
Calcium: 31 mg	Total Fat: 5 g (22% fat cals)	Saturated Fat: 0.5 g

---

EXCHANGES, PER SERVING (1 WAFFLE): 2 Starch; 1 Fat.

2

Eggs and Soufflés

Eggs are relatively low in calories and high in protein. While both the white
and yolk contribute to the high protein content, the yolk also contains
fat and cholesterol; the whites furnish riboflavin (vitamin B$_2$).
Liquid egg substitutes–used often in this cookbook–
are derived from egg whites and are essentially free of fat and cholesterol.
They are best used in cooked recipes and for the partial replacement of eggs
in omelets and soufflés. High in nutrients, both eggs and egg substitutes
are important foods for individuals who must watch
the amount of milk products in their diets.

Whether soft-cooked, poached, scrambled, or made into a flavorful omelet,
the wonderfully versatile egg is perfect for breakfast, brunch, or lunch.
And when whipped into an elegant soufflé or quiche,
eggs make an equally satisfying dinner entrée,
as well as a delightfully different side dish.

Scrambled Eggs

Yield: 4 servings
Prep. time: 10 minutes

3 eggs, at room
  temperature

¾ cup egg whites

2 tablespoons
  reduced-lactose milk

Black pepper to taste

1 tablespoon low-fat
  nondairy margarine

An easy-to-make breakfast.

1. In a small bowl, combine the eggs, egg whites, milk, and black pepper. Mix thoroughly with a fork.

2. In a small skillet, melt the margarine over medium heat. Reduce the heat to low and add the egg mixture. Cook, stirring constantly, until the desired consistency is reached, about 5 minutes. Serve immediately.

NUTRITIONAL FACTS PER SERVING

Calories: 80   Protein: 7 g   Carbohydrates: 1 g
Calcium: 34 mg   Total Fat: 4 g (45% fat cals)   Saturated Fat: 1.9 g

EXCHANGES, PER SERVING: 1 Medium Fat Meat.

Scrambled Eggs With Tofu

Yield: 6 servings
Prep. time: 10 minutes

1 pound soft tofu

1 egg, lightly beaten

½ cup egg substitute

2 tablespoons low-fat
  nondairy margarine

½ teaspoon minced garlic

Black pepper to taste

Not the usual scrambled eggs, this dish demonstrates the flavor-absorbing quality of tofu.

1. Squeeze the tofu dry by pressing it between a few layers of cheesecloth until the excess water has been removed. Place the tofu in a small bowl and mash it.

2. In a separate bowl, combine the egg and egg substitute; beat thoroughly with a fork.

3. In a large skillet, melt the margarine over medium heat. Add the garlic and sauté until lightly browned. Add the mashed tofu and the egg mixture, and stir. Add the black pepper and stir again.

4. Cover the skillet and cook the eggs for 2 minutes. Turn the eggs and cook for 2 more minutes; be careful not to overcook. Serve immediately.

NUTRITIONAL FACTS PER SERVING

Calories: 101   Protein: 7 g   Carbohydrates: 1.2 g
Calcium: 105 mg   Total Fat: 4.6 g (40% fat cals)   Saturated Fat: 1.6 g

EXCHANGES, PER SERVING: 1 Medium Fat Meat.

Vegetable Omelet

A colorful dish. When served with baked potatoes, it is a complete meal.

Yield: 2 servings
Prep. time: 15 minutes

1. In a small skillet, heat the olive oil over medium heat. Add the green pepper, green onion, and mushrooms, and cook until the vegetables are browned and soft.

2. In a small bowl, combine the egg and egg substitute; season with black pepper and beat thoroughly with a fork. Pour over the hot vegetables.

3. Cover the skillet, reduce the heat to low, and cook the eggs until set. Serve immediately.

1 teaspoon olive oil

1/4 cup chopped green pepper

1 green onion, chopped

4 medium mushrooms, sliced

1 egg

1/2 cup egg substitute

Black pepper to taste

NUTRITIONAL FACTS PER SERVING

Calories: 120   Protein: 11 g   Carbohydrates: 1 g
Calcium: 64 mg   Total Fat: 7 g (53% fat cals)   Saturated Fat: 1.5 g

EXCHANGES, PER SERVING: 1 1/2 Medium Fat Meat.

Omelet Soufflé

An attractive entrée that is ideal for a special luncheon.

Yield: 4 servings
Prep. time: 15 minutes
Baking time: 5 minutes

1. Preheat the oven to 350°F.

2. In a large bowl, combine the egg yolks, egg substitute, and soymilk; beat thoroughly with a fork. In a separate bowl, beat the egg whites until stiff. Fold the egg whites into the egg-yolk mixture.

3. In a small skillet, melt the margarine over medium heat. Reduce the heat to low and add the egg mixture. Cook the eggs for 5 minutes.

4. Transfer the skillet to the oven and bake the eggs for 5 minutes.

5. Remove the eggs from the oven and transfer to a serving plate. Serve with powdered sugar or jam.

3 eggs, separated

1/4 cup egg substitute

1/4 cup reduced-fat soymilk

1 tablespoon nondairy margarine

NUTRITIONAL FACTS PER SERVING

Calories: 66   Protein: 6 g   Carbohydrates: 0.5 g
Calcium: 25 mg   Total Fat: 4 g (55% fat cals)   Saturated Fat: 1.3 g

EXCHANGES, PER SERVING: 1 Medium Fat Meat.

Shirred Eggs

Yield: 4 servings
Prep. time: 5 minutes
Baking time: 6–8 minutes

4 eggs

4 teaspoons nondairy cream

1/8 teaspoon paprika, as garnish

A classic brunch treat.

1. Preheat the oven to 350°F. Lightly coat 4 small ramekins with nonstick cooking spray.

2. Carefully break each egg into a ramekin. Place 1 teaspoon nondairy cream on top of each egg. Place the eggs in the oven and bake until the yolks are set, about 6 to 8 minutes.

3. Remove the eggs from the oven and sprinkle with the paprika. Serve with cooked asparagus.

NUTRITIONAL FACTS PER SERVING

Calories: 89	Protein: 6 g	Carbohydrates: 1 g
Calcium: 30 mg	Total Fat: 7 g (71% fat cals)	Saturated Fat: 2 g

EXCHANGES, PER SERVING: 1 Medium Fat Meat; 1/2 Fat.

Broccoli Soufflé

Yield: 4 servings
Prep. time: 10 minutes
Baking time: 45 minutes

2 tablespoons nondairy margarine

1 1/2 tablespoons all-purpose flour

1/2 cup soymilk

2 eggs, beaten

1/4 cup egg substitute

1 tablespoon chopped onion

Black pepper to taste

2 1/2 cups frozen chopped broccoli, thawed and drained

1/4 cup dairy-free bread crumbs

Chopped spinach or turnip greens also work well in this recipe.

1. Preheat the oven to 350°F. Lightly coat a 1 1/2-quart soufflé dish with nonstick cooking spray.

2. In a large skillet, melt the margarine over medium heat. Remove the skillet from the heat and add the flour; stir until smooth. Add the soymilk, eggs, egg substitute, onion, and black pepper; stir. Add the broccoli and stir. Pour the broccoli mixture into the soufflé dish and sprinkle with the bread crumbs. Place the dish in the oven and bake until the soufflé is set, about 45 minutes.

3. Remove the soufflé from the oven and serve immediately.

NUTRITIONAL FACTS PER SERVING

Calories: 141	Protein: 10 g	Carbohydrates: 9 g
Calcium: 9 mg	Total Fat: 7 g (45% fat cals)	Saturated Fat: 1.2 g

EXCHANGES, PER SERVING: 1 Medium Fat Meat; 1 Vegetable.

Eggs Benedict

An elegant brunch or dinner dish when served with asparagus spears.

Yield: 6 servings
Prep. time: 20 minutes

1. In a small saucepan, heat the Egg-Free Hollandaise Sauce.

2. Toast the bread and cut each slice into a round. Place each round on a separate plate.

3. In a small skillet, heat the chicken stock over low heat. Add the chicken or turkey slices and heat for 5 minutes. Place 1 slice on each bread round.

4. In a large saucepan or large deep skillet, bring about 2 inches of water to a simmer over high heat. Reduce the heat, then crack the eggs open and carefully drop the yolks and whites into the water. Simmer the eggs until the yolks reach the desired consistency, about 3 to 5 minutes.

5. Remove the eggs from the water with a slotted spoon and place 1 on top of each slice of chicken or turkey breast. Drizzle each egg with 1 tablespoon of the warm Egg-Free Hollandaise Sauce. Serve immediately.

6 tablespoons Egg-Free Hollandaise Sauce (see page 73)

6 slices dairy-free white or whole wheat bread

¼ cup chicken stock

6 slices cooked chicken or turkey breast (about 1 ounce each)

6 eggs

NUTRITIONAL FACTS PER SERVING

Calories: 230	Protein: 16 g	Carbohydrates: 14 g
Calcium: 69 mg	Total Fat: 9 g (35% fat cals)	Saturated Fat: 4 g

EXCHANGES, PER SERVING: 1 Very Lean Meat; 1 Medium Fat Meat; 1 Starch; 1 Fat.

Onion Mushroom Quiche

Yield: 4 servings
Prep. time: 10 minutes
Baking time: 20 minutes

1 cup cooked brown rice

2 green onions, chopped

¼ cup cooked mushrooms

½ cup grated nondairy Cheddar cheese

1½ cups soymilk

2 eggs

½ cup egg substitute

Black pepper to taste

Serve with cooked broccoli for a colorful, balanced meal.

1. Preheat the oven to 350°F. Lightly coat four 4-inch custard dishes with nonstick cooking spray.

2. In each custard dish, place ¼ cup of the rice; press down lightly with a spoon. Over the rice, sprinkle the green onion, mushrooms, and cheese. In a medium bowl, combine the soymilk, eggs, egg substitute, and black pepper; beat thoroughly with a fork. Pour ¼ of the egg mixture into each custard dish. Bake until set, about 20 minutes.

3. Remove the quiches from the oven and serve immediately.

NUTRITIONAL FACTS PER SERVING

Calories: 145	Protein: 14 g	Carbohydrates: 8 g
Calcium: 110 mg	Total Fat: 6 g (37% fat cals)	Saturated Fat: 1.5 g

EXCHANGES, PER SERVING: ½ Very Lean Meat; 1 Medium Fat Meat; ½ Starch.

Carrot Soufflé

Yield: 8 servings
Prep. time: 15 minutes
Baking time: 30 minutes

4 cups cooked sliced carrots, puréed and cooled to room temperature

¼ cup brown sugar

1 tablespoon low-fat nondairy margarine

½ teaspoon grated lemon rind

¼ teaspoon ground nutmeg

4 eggs, separated

A versatile, delicious, and unusual side dish, perfect with chicken or fish.

1. Preheat the oven to 350°F. Lightly coat a 1-quart soufflé dish with nonstick cooking spray.

2. In a large bowl, combine the carrots with the brown sugar, margarine, lemon rind, and nutmeg; mix well. In a small bowl, lightly beat the egg yolks; add to the carrot mixture and mix gently. In a medium bowl, beat the egg whites until stiff; fold carefully into the carrot mixture. Pour the carrot mixture into the soufflé dish. Place the dish in the oven and bake until the soufflé is set, about 30 minutes.

3. Remove the soufflé from the oven and serve immediately.

NUTRITIONAL FACTS PER SERVING

Calories: 90	Protein: 4 g	Carbohydrates: 11 g
Calcium: 27 mg	Total Fat: 3 g (30% fat cals)	Saturated Fat: 1 g

EXCHANGES, PER SERVING: ½ Vegetable; ½ Starch; ½ Fat.

Chicken Soufflé

A great way to use leftover chicken and an especially nutritious meal when served with a salad or a green vegetable.

Yield: 4 servings
Prep. time: 10 minutes
Baking time: 45 minutes

1. Preheat the oven to 350F. Lightly coat a 1$\frac{1}{2}$-quart soufflé dish with nonstick cooking spray.

2. In a large bowl, combine the mashed potatoes, egg yolks, and egg substitute; beat well. Add the chicken, onion, and parsley, and mix. In a separate bowl, beat the egg whites until stiff; fold into the chicken mixture. Pour the chicken mixture into the soufflé dish. Place the dish in the oven and bake until the soufflé is set, about 45 minutes.

3. Remove the soufflé from the oven and serve immediately.

2 cups instant mashed potatoes, prepared with water and nondairy margarine and cooled to room temperature

2 eggs, separated

$\frac{1}{4}$ cup egg substitute

1 cup chopped or coarsely ground cooked chicken, white meat (meat or fish can be substituted)

1 tablespoon minced onion

1 tablespoon chopped fresh parsley

NUTRITIONAL FACTS PER SERVING

Calories: 148   Protein: 18 g   Carbohydrates: 10 g
Calcium: 43 mg   Total Fat: 3 g (18% fat cals)   Saturated Fat: 2 g

---

EXCHANGES, PER SERVING: 2 Very Lean Meat; $\frac{1}{2}$ Medium Fat Meat; $\frac{1}{2}$ Starch.

3

Breads and Muffins

People on dairy-free diets do not have the protein in milk products available to them. Since legumes supply amino acids that complement those in grains, the combination of beans or peas with grain products such as breads and muffins is an important source of complete protein. Bread also supplies carbohydrates and B vitamins.

Homemade breads let you vary the ingredients according to your particular taste. And few meal accompaniments are as satisfying as fresh, aromatic homemade bread. When you make a loaf, or when you buy one, remember that it will stay fresh longer when kept wrapped at room temperature–not in the refrigerator!

Basic White Bread

Yield: 2 loaves
Prep. time: 1 hour 45 min.
Baking time: 30–40 minutes

6 cups all-purpose flour

2 packages active dry yeast

2 tablespoons sugar

¼ teaspoon salt

2 cups hot water

3 tablespoons nondairy
    margarine

1 teaspoon oil

An excellent sandwich bread that can be easily modified by adding minced onion, sesame seeds, or even finely chopped walnuts.

1. In a large bowl, combine 1 cup of the flour with the yeast, sugar, and salt; stir well. Add the water and margarine, and beat with an electric mixer at slow speed for 2 minutes. Add another cup of the flour and beat on high speed until the dough is stiff, about 1 minute. Stir in the remaining flour with a spoon.

2. Turn the dough out onto a floured surface and knead until smooth and elastic, about 8 to 10 minutes. Cover loosely with a clean towel and let rise in a warm (80°F) place for 20 minutes.

3. Lightly grease two 9-x-5-inch loaf pans. With floured hands, punch down the dough, divide it in half, and shape each piece into a loaf. Place the loaves in the pans and brush the tops lightly with the oil. Cover the pans loosely with clean towels and let stand in a warm place until the dough has doubled in bulk, about 1 hour.

4. Preheat the oven to 400°F. Place the loaves in the oven and bake until the tops are golden brown, about 30 to 40 minutes.

5. Remove the loaves from the oven and immediately turn them out onto a wire rack. Allow to cool before slicing.

NUTRITIONAL FACTS PER SLICE (¹⁄₁₆ LOAF)

Calories: 90	Protein: 2 g	Carbohydrates: 17 g
Calcium: 4 mg	Total Fat: 1 g (10% fat cals)	Saturated Fat: 0.2 g

---

EXCHANGES, PER SLICE (¹⁄₁₆ LOAF): 1 Starch.

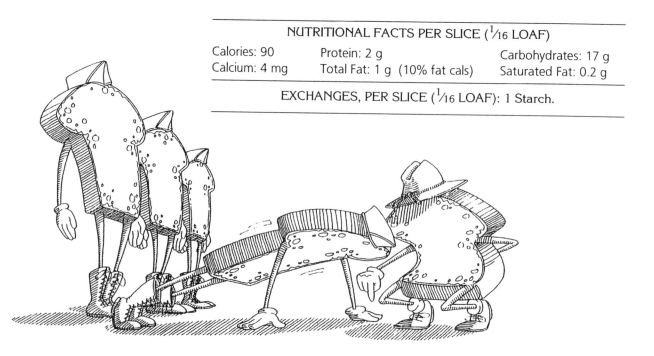

White Bread Plus

A full-bodied bread that toasts beautifully.

Yield: 2 loaves
Prep. time: 1 hour 50 min.
Baking time: 25–30 minutes

7 cups all-purpose flour

2 packages active dry yeast

3 tablespoons sugar

½ teaspoon salt

½ cup instant mashed
   potato flakes

2 cups very hot water

¼ cup nondairy margarine

1. In a large bowl, combine 2 cups of the flour with the yeast, sugar, and salt; stir well. In a separate bowl, combine the instant mashed potato flakes with the water and margarine; whip lightly with a fork. Add the wet ingredients to the dry ingredients and beat with an electric mixer at medium speed for 2 minutes. Add another 2 cups of the flour and beat on high speed until the dough is stiff, about 2 minutes. Stir in the remaining flour with a spoon.

2. Turn the dough out onto a floured surface and knead until smooth and elastic, about 8 to 10 minutes. Coat a clean large bowl with vegetable oil and place the dough in the bottom. Turn the dough over once to coat the top with oil. Cover the bowl loosely with a clean towel and let stand in a warm (80°F) place until the dough has doubled in bulk, about 1 hour.

3. With floured hands, punch down the dough and turn it out onto a floured surface. Cover loosely with a clean towel and let rise 15 minutes.

4. Lightly grease two 9-x-5-inch loaf pans. With floured hands, divide the dough in half and shape each piece into a loaf. Place the loaves in the pans, cover the pans loosely with clean towels, and let stand in a warm place until the dough has doubled in bulk, about 1 hour.

5. Preheat the oven to 400°F. Place the loaves in the oven and bake until the tops are golden brown, about 25 to 30 minutes.

6. Remove the loaves from the oven and immediately turn them out onto a wire rack. Allow to cool before slicing.

NUTRITIONAL FACTS PER SLICE (¹⁄₁₆ LOAF)

Calories: 107	Protein: 2.6 g	Carbohydrates: 20 g
Calcium: 5 mg	Total Fat: 2 g (17% fat cals)	Saturated Fat: 0.3 g

EXCHANGES, PER SLICE (¹⁄₁₆ LOAF): 1 Starch; ½ Fat.

Fat-Free White Bread

Yield: 1 loaf
Prep. time: 1 hour
Baking time: 25 minutes

1 package active dry yeast

1 tablespoon sugar

¼ cup warm water

1 cup orange juice

¼ teaspoon salt

¼ teaspoon baking soda

2½ cups all-purpose flour

2 tablespoons cornmeal

A basic nonfat, all-purpose, low-calorie bread. Serve it with a hearty vegetable soup for a wonderful meal.

1. In a large bowl, dissolve the yeast and sugar in the water. Let stand until foamy, about 5 minutes.

2. When the yeast has softened, add the orange juice and salt; stir. In a separate bowl, combine the baking soda with 1 cup of the flour. Add to the yeast mixture and beat well for 2 minutes. Stir in the remaining flour to make a stiff dough.

3. Lightly coat a 9-x-5-inch loaf pan with nonstick cooking spray and sprinkle with cornmeal, shaking off the excess. Spoon in the dough and sprinkle the top with the 2 tablespoons cornmeal. Cover the pan loosely with a clean towel and let stand in a warm (80°F) place until the dough has doubled in bulk, about 45 minutes.

4. Preheat the oven to 400°F. Place the loaf in the oven and bake until the top is golden brown, about 25 minutes.

5. Remove the loaf from the oven and immediately turn it out onto a wire rack. Allow to cool before slicing.

NUTRITIONAL FACTS PER SLICE (¹⁄₁₆ LOAF)

Calories: 63	Protein: 2 g	Carbohydrates: 14 g
Calcium: 3 mg	Total Fat: 0 g	Saturated Fat: 0 g

EXCHANGES, PER SLICE (¹⁄₁₆ LOAF): 1 Starch.

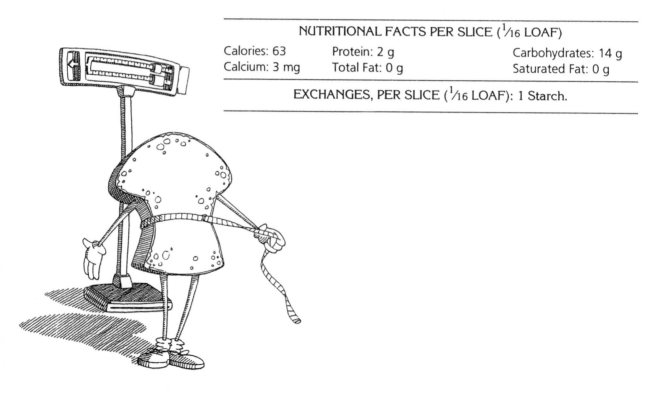

Rye Bread

An outstanding bread for sliced-meat sandwiches.

Yield: *2 loaves*
Prep. time: *3 hours*
Baking time: *40 minutes*

2 packages active dry yeast

6 cups rye flour

1/2 cup instant mashed potato flakes

2 cups hot water

1/2 cup sugar

1/4 cup oil

1/2 teaspoon salt

1. In a large bowl, combine the yeast with 2 cups of the flour; mix well. In a separate bowl, combine the instant mashed potato flakes with the water; whip lightly with a fork. Add the sugar, oil, and salt; mix well. Add the wet ingredients to the dry ingredients and beat with an electric mixer at medium speed for 2 minutes, scraping the bowl occasionally. Add another 2 cups of the flour and beat at high speed for 2 minutes, scraping the bowl. Using a spoon, stir in as much of the remaining flour as necessary to make a stiff dough.

2. Turn the dough out onto a surface sprinkled with rye flour and knead until smooth and elastic, about 8 to 10 minutes. Coat a clean large bowl with oil and place the dough in the bottom. Turn the dough over once to coat the top with oil. Cover the bowl loosely with a clean towel and let stand in a warm (80°F) place until the dough has doubled in bulk, about 1 1/2 hours.

3. With a floured fist, punch down the dough. Cover the bowl loosely with a clean towel and let stand in a warm place until the dough has doubled in bulk, about 30 to 45 minutes.

4. Lightly grease two 9-x-5-inch loaf pans. With floured hands, divide the dough in half and shape each piece into a loaf. Place the loaves in the pans.

5. Preheat the oven to 350°F. Place the loaves in the oven and bake until the tops are well browned, about 40 minutes.

6. Remove the loaves from the oven and immediately turn them out onto a wire rack. Allow to cool before slicing.

NUTRITIONAL FACTS PER SLICE (1/16 LOAF)

Calories: 93	Protein: 2.5 g	Carbohydrates: 17 g
Calcium: 7.8 mg	Total Fat: 2 g (19% fat cals)	Saturated Fat: 0.3 g

---

EXCHANGES, PER SLICE (1/16 LOAF): 1 Starch.

Multi-Grain Bread

Yield: 1 loaf
Prep. time: 20 minutes
Baking time: 50 minutes

1 package active dry yeast

½ cup lukewarm water

2 tablespoons molasses

2 tablespoons honey

1 tablespoon oil

1 cup orange juice

¾ cup whole wheat flour

¾ cup rye flour

¼ cup rolled oats

¼ cup cornmeal

½ teaspoon salt

2 cups all-purpose flour

A heavy, flavorful bread that is ideal with stews and goulash.

1. In a large bowl, combine the yeast with the water, molasses, honey, and oil. Add the orange juice and stir well. Add the whole wheat flour, rye flour, rolled oats, cornmeal, salt, and 1 cup of the all-purpose flour; mix thoroughly. Cover the bowl loosely with a clean towel and let stand in a warm (80°F) place until the dough has doubled in bulk, about 1½ hours.

2. Turn the dough out onto a surface sprinkled with the remaining all-purpose flour and knead until smooth and elastic, about 8 to 10 minutes. Add more all-purpose flour if necessary.

3. Lightly coat a 9-x-5-inch loaf pan with nonstick cooking spray. With floured hands, shape the dough into a loaf and place in the pan. Cover the pan loosely with a clean towel and let stand in a warm place until the dough has doubled in bulk, about 45 minutes.

4. Preheat the oven to 400°F. Place the loaf in the oven and bake for 20 minutes. Then lower the temperature to 350°F and bake until the top is well browned, about 30 minutes more.

5. Remove the loaf from the oven and immediately turn it out onto a wire rack. Allow to cool before slicing.

NUTRITIONAL FACTS PER SLICE (¹⁄₁₆ LOAF)

Calories: 146	Protein: 4 g	Carbohydrates: 31 g
Calcium: 13 mg	Total Fat: 1 g (6% fat cals)	Saturated Fat: 0.2 g

---

EXCHANGES, PER SLICE (¹⁄₁₆ LOAF): 2 Starch.

Oatmeal Bread

A good source of fiber, this bread is an example of what is not readily available from commercial bakeries.

1. In a large bowl, pour the water over the rolled oats. Add the molasses, oil, and salt, and mix. In a separate large bowl, combine the yeast with 2 cups of the flour; stir well. Add the wet ingredients to the dry ingredients and beat with an electric mixer at medium speed for 2 minutes, scraping the bowl. Add another cup of the flour and beat at high speed for 2 minutes, scraping the bowl frequently. Stir in the remaining flour with a spoon.

2. Turn the dough out onto a lightly floured surface and knead until smooth and elastic, about 8 to 10 minutes. Coat a clean large bowl with vegetable oil and place the dough in the bottom. Turn the dough over once to coat the top with oil. Cover the bowl loosely with a clean towel and let stand in a warm (80°F) place until the dough has doubled in bulk, about 1 hour.

3. Lightly grease two 9-x-5-inch loaf pans. With floured hands, punch down the dough, divide it in half, and shape each piece into a loaf. Place the loaves in the pans. Cover the pans loosely with clean towels and let stand in a warm place until the dough has doubled in bulk, about 1 hour.

4. Preheat the oven to 375°F. Place the loaves in the oven and bake until the tops are browned, about 45 minutes.

5. Remove the loaves from the oven and immediately turn them out onto a wire rack. Allow to cool before slicing.

Yield: 2 loaves
Prep. time: 1 hour 30 min.
Baking time: 45 minutes

$2\frac{1}{2}$ cups hot water

2 cups rolled oats

$\frac{1}{2}$ cup molasses

$\frac{1}{4}$ cup oil

$\frac{1}{4}$ tablespoon salt

2 packages active dry yeast

6 cups all-purpose flour

NUTRITIONAL FACTS PER SLICE ($\frac{1}{16}$ LOAF)

Calories: 135	Protein: 3.2 g	Carbohydrates: 25 g
Calcium: 15 mg	Total Fat: 2 g (13% fat cals)	Saturated Fat: 0.2 g

EXCHANGES, PER SLICE ($\frac{1}{16}$ LOAF): $1\frac{1}{2}$ Starch.

Challah

Yield: 2 loaves
Prep. time: 2 hours 30 min.
Baking time: 45 minutes

2 packages active dry yeast

2 tablespoons sugar

2 cups warm water

½ teaspoon salt

6 cups all-purpose flour

3 eggs

3 tablespoons oil

1 tablespoon water

A beautiful, golden-colored bread for the holiday table. If any is left over, use is to make French Toast (see page 14).

1. In a medium bowl, dissolve the yeast and sugar in the warm water. Let stand until foamy, about 5 minutes. Add the salt.

2. In a large bowl, sift the flour. In a small bowl, beat the eggs; reserve 1 tablespoon to use as a glaze in step 5. To the small bowl, add the oil and stir well. Add the egg mixture to the yeast mixture, then quickly add the combined mixture to the flour, stirring until a soft ball has formed.

3. Turn the dough out onto a lightly floured surface and knead until smooth and elastic, about 8 to 10 minutes. Coat a clean large bowl with vegetable oil and place the dough in the bottom. Turn the dough over once to coat the top with oil. Cover the bowl loosely with a clean towel and let stand in a warm (80°F) place until the dough has doubled in bulk, about 50 minutes.

4. Lightly grease two 9-x-5-inch loaf pans. With floured hands, punch down the dough. Turn the dough out onto a lightly floured surface and knead for about 2 minutes. Divide the dough into 6 equal pieces. Roll each piece into a fat rope about 12 inches long. Braid 3 of the ropes loosely together, then braid the remaining 3 ropes loosely together. Place the braided loaves in the pans, cover loosely with clean towels, and let stand in a warm place until doubled in bulk, about 30 minutes.

5. Preheat the oven to 400°F. In a small bowl, combine the reserved beaten egg with the 1 tablespoon water; brush on the braided loaves in the pans. Place the loaves in the oven and bake until the tops are golden brown, about 45 minutes.

6. Remove the loaves from the oven and immediately turn them out onto a wire rack. Allow to cool before slicing.

NUTRITIONAL FACTS PER SLICE (¹⁄₁₆ LOAF)

Calories: 98	Protein: 2.8 g	Carbohydrates: 17 g
Calcium: 6.5 mg	Total Fat: 2 g (18% fat cals)	Saturated Fat: 0.4 g

EXCHANGES, PER SLICE (¹⁄₁₆ LOAF): 1 Starch.

Cornbread

Great with chicken dishes, in a stuffing, or with jam and coffee. Try toasting a thin slice and placing it in the bottom of a bowl of vegetable soup.

1. Preheat the oven to 450°F. Lightly grease an 8-inch-square cake pan.

2. In a large bowl, sift together the cornmeal, rice flour, sugar, baking powder, and salt. Add the eggs, water, and oil. Mix just until the dry ingredients are moistened.

3. Pour the batter into the pan. Place the loaf in the oven and bake until a cake tester inserted in the center comes out clean, about 20 minutes.

4. Remove the loaf from the oven and allow it to cool for 5 minutes. Cut into 9 squares and remove from the pan. Serve warm.

Yield: 1 loaf
Prep. time: 10 minutes
Baking time: 20 minutes

1½ cups cornmeal

3 tablespoons rice flour

1 tablespoon sugar

1 teaspoon baking powder

¼ teaspoon salt

3 eggs

1½ cups water

2 tablespoons oil

NUTRITIONAL FACTS PER SLICE (¹⁄₁₆ LOAF)

Calories: 130	Protein: 2 g	Carbohydrates: 16 g
Calcium: 11 mg	Total Fat: 5 g (35% fat cals)	Saturated Fat: 1 g

EXCHANGES, PER SLICE (¹⁄₁₆ LOAF): 1 Starch; 1 Fat.

Date Nut Muffins

A great, chewy after-school treat.

1. Preheat the oven to 375°F. Lightly coat 12 muffin cups with nonstick cooking spray.

2. In a large bowl, sprinkle the baking soda over the dates. Add the boiling water. Add the flour, sugar, margarine, and nuts, and mix until moistened.

3. Fill the muffin cups ²⁄₃ full. Place the muffins in the oven and bake until a tester inserted in the center comes out clean, 20 to 25 minutes.

4. Remove the muffins from the oven and remove from the cups. Serve warm.

Yield: 12 muffins
Prep. time: 20 minutes
Baking time: 20–25 minutes

1 teaspoon baking soda

1 cup chopped dates

¾ cup boiling water

1½ cups flour

½ cup sugar

¼ cup low-fat nondairy margarine

¼ cup chopped almonds

NUTRITIONAL FACTS PER MUFFIN

Calories: 140	Protein: 3 g	Carbohydrates: 19 g
Calcium: 34 mg	Total Fat: 3 g (19% fat cals)	Saturated Fat: 0.3 g

EXCHANGES, PER MUFFIN: 1 Starch; ½ Fat.

Boston Brown Bread

Yield: 1 loaf
Prep. time: 20 minutes
Baking time: 1 hour 40 min.

¾ cup rye flour

¾ cup cornmeal

¾ cup whole wheat flour

2 teaspoons baking soda

½ teaspoon salt

1½ cups mashed soft tofu

1 tablespoon water

1 cup soymilk

½ cup molasses

1 tablespoon lemon juice

An excellent traditional accompaniment for baked bean side dishes.

1. Lightly grease a 9-x-5-inch loaf pan.

2. In a large bowl, mix together the rye flour, cornmeal, whole wheat flour, baking soda, and salt. In a blender, purée the tofu with the water. Add the soymilk, molasses, and lemon juice to the blender and mix. Add the liquid ingredients to the dry ingredients and mix well.

3. Fill the pan ⅔ full with the batter. Tightly seal the top of the pan with foil. Place the pan on a steamer rack inside a large pot or kettle that is at least 3 inches taller than the pan. Pour enough boiling water into the pot to reach halfway up the sides of the pan. Cover the pot with a lid, place the pot on the stove, and keep the water boiling. Steam the loaf for 1½ hours, adding more boiling water as necessary to maintain a constant level around the pan.

4. Preheat the oven to 300°F. Remove the pan from the pot and remove the foil cover. Place the pan in the oven for 10 minutes to dry the bread slightly.

5. Remove the loaf from the oven and immediately turn it out onto a wire rack. Allow to cool before slicing.

NUTRITIONAL FACTS PER SLICE (1/16 LOAF)

Calories: 70	Protein: 1 g	Carbohydrates: 15 g
Calcium: 17 mg	Total Fat: 1 g (13% fat cals)	Saturated Fat: 0.1 g

EXCHANGES, PER SLICE (1/16 LOAF): 1 Starch.

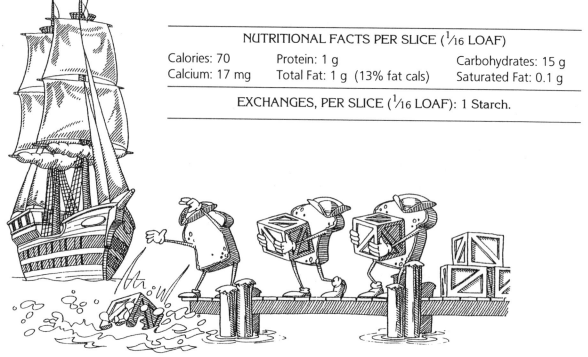

Orange Nut Bread

Makes the most delicious nondairy cream cheese sandwiches!

1. Preheat the oven to 350°F. Lightly grease a 9-x-5-inch loaf pan.

2. In a large bowl, sift together the oat flour, sugar, baking powder, baking soda, and salt. Add the walnuts, orange juice, oil, and orange rind. Mix just until the dry ingredients are moistened.

3. Pour the batter into the pan. Place the loaf in the oven and bake until a cake tester inserted in the center comes out clean, about 1 hour.

4. Remove the loaf from the oven and immediately turn it out onto a wire rack. Allow to cool before slicing.

Yield: 1 loaf
Prep. time: 15 minutes
Baking time: 1 hour

2¼ cups oat flour

¾ cup sugar

4 teaspoons baking powder

¼ teaspoon baking soda

¼ teaspoon salt

1 cup chopped walnuts

¾ cup orange juice

2 tablespoons oil

1 tablespoon grated orange rind

NUTRITIONAL FACTS PER SLICE (1/16 LOAF)

Calories: 144   Protein: 4 g   Carbohydrates: 16 g
Calcium: 12 mg   Total Fat: 2 g (13% fat cals)   Saturated Fat: 0.5 g

EXCHANGES, PER SLICE (1/16 LOAF): 1 Starch.

Pumpkin Bread

A treat for Halloween and Thanksgiving, this cakelike bread is delightful any day of the year with a cup of tea.

1. Preheat the oven to 350°F. Lightly grease two 9-x-5-inch loaf pans.

2. In a large bowl, combine the pumpkin, sugar, brown sugar, and oil; mix well. In a separate bowl, sift together the flour, baking soda, spice, and salt. Add the dry ingredients to the wet ingredients and mix just until the dry ingredients are moistened. Fold in the dates.

3. Pour half the batter into each pan. Place the loaves in the oven and bake until a cake tester inserted in the center comes out clean, about 1 hour.

4. Remove the loaves from the oven and immediately turn them out onto a wire rack. Allow to cool before slicing.

Yield: 2 loaves
Prep. time: 15 minutes
Baking time: 1 hour

1-pound can pumpkin

1 cup sugar

1 cup firmly packed brown sugar

½ cup oil

2½ cups all-purpose flour

2 teaspoons baking soda

2 teaspoons pumpkin pie spice

¼ teaspoon salt

½ cup chopped dates

NUTRITIONAL FACTS PER SLICE (1/16 LOAF)

Calories: 120   Protein: 1 g   Carbohydrates: 22 g
Calcium: 13 mg   Total Fat: 4 g (30% fat cals)   Saturated Fat: 0.3 g

EXCHANGES, PER SLICE (1/16 LOAF): 1½ Starch; ½ Fat.

Dinner Rolls

Yield: 24 rolls
Prep. time: 3 hours
Baking time: 15 minutes

3¼ cups all-purpose flour

1 package active dry yeast

½ cup sugar

½ teaspoon salt

¼ cup nondairy margarine,
  melted

2 tablespoons instant
  mashed potato flakes

1 cup hot water

A classic roll for any meal, the texture and taste can be altered easily.
For example, I like to add poppy seeds to the batter.

1. In a large bowl, combine 1 cup of the flour with the yeast, sugar, and salt. Add the margarine and instant mashed potato flakes, and stir. Add the hot water and beat with an electric mixer at medium speed for 2 minutes, scraping the bowl frequently. Add another cup of the flour and beat at high speed for 2 minutes. Add the remaining flour and mix thoroughly with a spoon. Cover the bowl loosely with a clean towel and place in the refrigerator for at least 2 hours.

2. Lightly grease 2 large baking sheets. Divide the dough into 24 equal pieces and shape each piece into a roll. Arrange 2 inches apart on the baking sheet. Cover the baking sheet loosely with a clean towel and let stand in a warm place until the dough has doubled in bulk, about 45 minutes.

3. Preheat the oven to 350°F. Place the rolls in the oven and bake until lightly browned, about 15 minutes.

4. Remove the rolls from the oven and remove from the baking sheet. Serve warm.

NUTRITIONAL FACTS PER ROLL

Calories: 80	Protein: 2 g	Carbohydrates: 14 g
Calcium: 4 mg	Total Fat: 2 g (23% fat cals)	Saturated Fat: 0.2 g

EXCHANGES, PER ROLL: 1 Starch.

Sweet Rolls

An old-timer but still a sensational treat at coffee-break time.

Yield: 36 rolls
Prep. time: 2 hours 30 min.
Baking time: 10 minutes

1. In a large bowl, combine 1 cup of the flour with the yeast, $\frac{1}{2}$ cup sugar, and salt. Add the margarine and instant mashed potato flakes, and stir. Add the hot water and beat with an electric mixer at medium speed for 2 minutes, scraping the bowl frequently. Add another cup of the flour and beat at high speed for 2 minutes. Add the remaining flour and mix thoroughly with a spoon. Cover the bowl loosely with a clean towel and place in the refrigerator for at least 2 hours.

2. Preheat the oven to 350°F. Lightly grease 3 large baking sheets. Divide the dough in half and roll out each piece into a 9-x-18-inch rectangle. Sprinkle each rectangle with half of the $\frac{1}{4}$ cup sugar and the cinnamon, and roll up like a jelly roll. Brush each roll with the egg white and cut into 1-inch slices. Arrange the slices 2 inches apart on the baking sheet. Place the rolls in the oven and bake until lightly browned, about 10 minutes.

3. Remove the rolls from the oven and remove from the baking sheet. Serve warm.

3¼ cups all-purpose flour

1 package active dry yeast

$\frac{1}{2}$ cup sugar

$\frac{1}{2}$ teaspoon salt

$\frac{1}{4}$ cup nondairy margarine, melted

2 tablespoons instant mashed potato flakes

1 cup hot water

$\frac{1}{4}$ cup sugar

1 teaspoon cinnamon

1 egg white

NUTRITIONAL FACTS PER ROLL

Calories: 85	Protein: 1.5 g	Carbohydrates: 15 g
Calcium: 3 mg	Total Fat: 1.5 g (16% fat cals)	Saturated Fat: 1 g

EXCHANGES, PER ROLL: 1 Starch.

Bagels

Yield: 24 bagels
Prep. time: 1 hour 30 min.
Baking time: 20–25 minutes

2 packages active dry yeast

1½ cups warm water

4 cups all-purpose flour

2 tablespoons sugar

1 tablespoon nondairy margarine

½ teaspoon salt

Perennial Sunday morning favorites. Try serving them with nondairy cheeses and smoked fish.

1. In a large bowl, dissolve the yeast in ½ cup of the warm water. Add the remaining water, 2 cups of the flour, and the sugar, margarine, and salt. Beat until smooth. Add the remaining flour to make a moderately stiff dough.

2. Turn the dough out onto a lightly floured surface and knead until smooth and elastic, about 10 minutes. Cover the dough loosely with a clean towel and let rest for 20 minutes.

3. Roll out the dough to a ¾-inch thickness. Using a floured 3-inch doughnut cutter, cut out 24 bagels. Place the bagels on ungreased baking sheets, cover them loosely with clean towels, and let rest for another 20 minutes.

4. In a large saucepan, add 1 tablespoon sugar and ½ teaspoon salt to 2½ quarts water; bring to a boil. Drop 2 to 4 bagels into the boiling water and simmer for 2 minutes. Flip the bagels over and simmer another 2 minutes. Remove the bagels from the water and place them on paper towels to drain. Repeat with the remaining bagels.

5. Preheat the oven to 425°F. Lightly grease a clean baking sheet. Transfer the drained bagels to the baking sheet, place in the oven, and bake until golden brown, about 20 to 25 minutes.

6. Remove the bagels from the oven and immediately place them on a wire rack. Serve warm or toasted.

NUTRITIONAL FACTS PER BAGEL

Calories: 150	Protein: 4 g	Carbohydrates: 30 g
Calcium: 7 mg	Total Fat: 1 g (6% fat cals)	Saturated Fat: 0.3 g

---

EXCHANGES, PER BAGEL: 2 Starch.

Oat Muffins

Excellent served warm with jam.

1. Preheat oven to 400°F. Lightly coat 12 muffin cups with cooking spray.

2. In a large bowl, sift together the oat flour, sugar, baking powder, and salt. In a medium bowl, pour the hot water over the raisins; add the oil. Add the wet ingredients to the dry ingredients and mix just until the dry ingredients are moistened.

3. Fill the muffin cups $^2/_3$ full with the batter. Place the muffins in the oven and bake until a cake tester inserted in the center comes out clean, about 25 minutes.

4. Remove muffins from oven and remove from cups. Serve warm.

Yield: 12 muffins
Prep. time: 20 minutes
Baking time: 25 minutes

2 cups oat flour

$^1/_2$ cup sugar

1$^1/_2$ teaspoons baking powder

$^1/_4$ teaspoon salt

1$^1/_4$ cups hot water

$^1/_2$ cup raisins

$^1/_4$ cup oil

NUTRITIONAL FACTS PER MUFFIN

Calories: 114	Protein: 2 g	Carbohydrates: 19 g
Calcium: 9 mg	Total Fat: 4 g (32% fat cals)	Saturated Fat: 0 g

EXCHANGES, PER MUFFIN: 1 Starch; 1 Fat.

Blueberry Muffins

Great for breakfast and easy to make!

1. Preheat oven to 425°F. Lightly coat 12 muffin cups with cooking spray.

2. In a large bowl, sift together the flour, sugar, and baking powder. In a separate bowl, combine the egg, soymilk, and margarine. Add the wet ingredients to the dry ingredients and mix just until the dry ingredients are moistened and the large lumps are gone. Fold in the blueberries.

3. Fill the muffin cups $^2/_3$ full with the batter. Place the muffins in the oven and bake until a cake tester inserted in the center comes out clean, about 25 minutes.

4. Remove muffins from oven and remove from cups. Serve warm.

Yield: 12 muffins
Prep. time: 20 minutes
Baking time: 25 minutes

2 cups all-purpose flour

$^1/_4$ cup sugar

2 teaspoons baking powder

1 egg, beaten

1 cup soymilk

2 tablespoons nondairy margarine, melted

1$^1/_2$ cups fresh or frozen blueberries

NUTRITIONAL FACTS PER MUFFIN

Calories: 139	Protein: 3 g	Carbohydrates: 26 g
Calcium: 16 mg	Total Fat: 3 g (19% fat cals)	Saturated Fat: 0.4 g

EXCHANGES, PER MUFFIN: 1 Starch; $^1/_2$ Fruit; $^1/_2$ Fat.

Oat Biscuits

Yield: 12 biscuits
Prep. time: 30 minutes
Baking time: 15–20 minutes

1 cup oat flour

1 tablespoon baking powder

1 tablespoon sugar

$\frac{1}{4}$ teaspoon salt

1 tablespoon nondairy
  margarine

$\frac{1}{8}$ cup cold water

Perfect with any dish, but especially good with creamed chicken.

1. Preheat the oven to 450°F.

2. In a large bowl, sift together the oat flour, baking powder, sugar, and salt. Cut the margarine into $\frac{1}{4}$-inch pieces and add to the dry ingredients. Add the cold water and stir gently to form a soft dough.

3. Turn the dough out onto a surface sprinkled with oat flour and knead lightly until smooth, about 1 minute. Roll out the dough to a $\frac{1}{2}$-inch thickness. Using a floured $1\frac{1}{2}$-inch biscuit or cookie cutter, cut out 12 rounds. Place the rounds on an ungreased baking sheet. Place the rounds in the oven and bake until golden brown, about 15 to 20 minutes.

4. Remove the biscuits from the oven and remove from the baking sheet. Serve warm.

NUTRITIONAL FACTS PER BISCUIT

Calories: 45	Protein: 1 g	Carbohydrates: 7 g
Calcium: 66 mg	Total Fat: 1.5 g (30% fat cals)	Saturated Fat: 0.3 g

---

EXCHANGES, PER BISCUIT: $\frac{1}{2}$ Starch.

4

Soups

The variety of soups is mind-boggling. Soups range from delicate consommés
to hearty creations that can serve as complete meals. They are a convenient way
to serve important foods such as vegetables, pasta, and fish–
ingredients that are highlighted in many of the following recipes.
Also offered in this section are a number of creamy soups
that use nondairy products such as tofu as thickeners.
Note that soups can be prepared in advance in large quantities,
and then kept in the refrigerator for about one week, or stored in the freezer.

Borscht

Yield: 4 servings
Prep. time: 1 hour 30 min.

1-pound can sliced beets,
  undrained

4 cups beef bouillon

2 cups shredded cabbage

½ cup chopped onion

½ cup chopped carrot

½ cup diced potato

2 tablespoons vinegar

¼ cup nondairy sour cream
  or nonpasteurized
  yogurt, as garnish

Especially refreshing when served cold, this unusual European version is slightly more full-bodied than the more conventional ones.

1. In a large saucepan, combine the beets, beet liquid, bouillon, cabbage, onions, carrots, potatoes, and vinegar. Bring to a boil over medium heat, then reduce the heat and simmer until the vegetables are tender, about 1 hour. Cool slightly.

2. Pour the mixture into a blender in small batches and liquify.

3. Return the mixture to the saucepan, reheat, and serve hot; or place in the refrigerator for at least 1 hour and serve cold. Garnish each serving with 1 tablespoon of the sour cream or yogurt.

NUTRITIONAL FACTS PER SERVING

Calories: 196	Protein: 8 g	Carbohydrates: 38 g
Calcium: 140 mg	Total Fat: 2.5 g (11% fat cals)	Saturated Fat: 0.8 g

---

EXCHANGES, PER SERVING: 2 Starch; 1 Vegetable; ½ Fat.

French Onion Soup

Yield: 6 servings
Prep. time: 1 hour 30 min.

1 tablespoon olive oil

6 large onions, thinly sliced

6 cups beef bouillon

⅓ cup red or white wine

3 slices dairy-free bread,
  toasted

¼ cup grated nondairy
  hard cheese such as
  Parmesan or Cheddar

A gourmet treat.

1. In a large saucepan, heat the olive oil over medium heat. Add the onions and sauté until limp. Add the bouillon and stir. Bring to a boil, then cover, reduce the heat, and simmer slowly for 30 minutes.

2. Preheat the oven to 350°F.

3. Add the wine to the soup and stir. Ladle into individual ovenproof soup bowls. Cut the bread slices in half and place 1 half in each bowl. Sprinkle each bowl with ⅙ of the grated cheese. Place in the oven until the cheese melts, about 3 minutes.

4. Remove from the oven and serve hot.

NUTRITIONAL FACTS PER SERVING

Calories: 160	Protein: 8 g	Carbohydrates: 13 g
Calcium: 165 mg	Total Fat: 4.5 g (25% fat cals)	Saturated Fat: 1.5 g

---

EXCHANGES, PER SERVING: ½ Meat; ½ Starch; 1 Vegetable; ½ Fat.

Onion Soup

A modification of a perennial favorite. I serve it with slices of toasted homemade white bread, placed in the bowls before the steaming soup is ladled in.

Yield: 4 servings
Prep. time: 1 hour

1 tablespoon olive oil

2 cups chopped onion

1 teaspoon minced garlic

5 cups water

$\frac{1}{2}$ cup white wine

Black pepper to taste

2 ounces firm tofu, drained

2 teaspoons olive oil

2 teaspoons grated nondairy Parmesan cheese

1. In a large saucepan, heat the 1 tablespoon of olive oil over medium heat. Add the onion and sauté until soft and translucent. Add the garlic and sauté for 3 more minutes. Add the water, white wine, and pepper. Bring to a boil, reduce the heat, and simmer for about 40 minutes.

2. Preheat the oven to 350°F. Lightly coat a baking sheet with nonstick cooking spray.

3. Cut the tofu into $\frac{1}{4}$-inch cubes and place in a small bowl. Add the 2 teaspoons of olive oil and toss the tofu to coat. Transfer to the baking sheet, place in the oven, and bake until crusty, about 5 minutes. Add to the soup.

4. Preheat the broiler. Remove the soup from the heat and ladle it into individual ovenproof soup bowls. Sprinkle $\frac{1}{2}$ teaspoon of the grated Parmesan in each bowl and place under the broiler. Broil until the cheese melts, about 1 minute. Serve immediately.

NUTRITIONAL FACTS PER SERVING

Calories: 110	Protein: 2.7 g	Carbohydrates: 9 g
Calcium: 57 mg	Total Fat: 6 g (49% fat cals)	Saturated Fat: 0.8 g

---

EXCHANGES, PER SERVING: 1 Vegetable; 1 Fat.

Fresh Vegetable Soup

Yield: 6 servings
Prep. time: 1 hour

4 cups chopped fresh
  tomato

2 cups reduced-fat chicken
  bouillon

1 cup sliced carrot

1 cup sliced celery

1 cup fresh green beans,
  cut into 1-inch lengths

1 cup chopped onion

½ teaspoon dried basil

½ teaspoon dried thyme

1 clove garlic, crushed

Black pepper to taste

1 tablespoon chopped fresh
  dill

A delicious dish that uses fresh vegetables and herbs. It is ideal served with freshly baked bread.

1. In a large saucepan, combine all the ingredients except the fresh dill. Bring to a boil over high heat, then cover, reduce the heat, and simmer until the vegetables are tender, about 40 minutes.

2. When ready to serve, add the dill. Serve hot.

NUTRITIONAL FACTS PER SERVING

Calories: 81   Protein: 3 g   Carbohydrates: 14 g
Calcium: 33 mg   Total Fat: 2 g (22% fat cals)   Saturated Fat: 0.3 g

EXCHANGES, PER SERVING: 1 Starch; ½ Fat.

Potato Bean Soup

An especially hearty soup, this makes an ideal meal when served with a salad.

1. In a large saucepan, place the potatoes in the water. Bring to a boil over high heat, then reduce the heat and simmer for about 15 minutes. Add the green beans and simmer until tender, about 15 minutes more.

2. In a small skillet, heat the oil over medium heat. Add the onion and garlic, and sauté until limp, about 5 minutes. Add to the potato mixture.

3. Season the soup with the black pepper and garnish with the parsley. Serve hot.

Yield: 6 servings
Prep. time: 45 minutes

1½ pounds potatoes, peeled and cut into 1-inch cubes

6 cups water

1 pound green beans, cut into 1-inch lengths

1 tablespoon oil

1 small onion, chopped

2 teaspoons minced garlic

Black pepper to taste

½ teaspoon chopped fresh parsley, as garnish

NUTRITIONAL FACTS PER SERVING

| Calories: 114 | Protein: 2.6 g | Carbohydrates: 22 g |
| Calcium: 33 mg | Total Fat: 2.6 g (21% fat cals) | Saturated Fat: 0.4 g |

EXCHANGES, PER SERVING: 1 Starch; ½ Fat; ½ Fruit.

Potato Leek Soup

A satisfying old-time cold-weather soup with a creamy consistency.

1. In a large saucepan, combine the water, potatoes, leeks, celery, dillweed, garlic, and black pepper. Bring to a boil over high heat, then reduce the heat and simmer until the potatoes are tender, about 20 minutes.

2. In a small skillet, melt the margarine over low heat. Add the cornstarch and cook, stirring constantly, until smooth, about 3 minutes. Gradually add the bouillon and stir until smooth. Add to the potato mixture and stir well.

3. Heat until hot and serve immediately.

Yield: 4 servings
Prep. time: 35 minutes

3 cups water

4 medium potatoes, peeled and diced

2 large leeks, thinly sliced

2 stalks celery, diced

1 teaspoon dried dillweed

1 teaspoon crushed garlic

Black pepper to taste

1 tablespoon nondairy margarine

1 tablespoon cornstarch

1 cup reduced-fat chicken bouillon

NUTRITIONAL FACTS PER SERVING

| Calories: 150 | Protein: 3.7 g | Carbohydrates: 28 g |
| Calcium: 20 mg | Total Fat: 3 g (18% fat cals) | Saturated Fat: 0.7 g |

EXCHANGES, PER SERVING: 1 Starch; ½ Fat; 1 Fruit.

Quick Cream of Corn Soup

Yield: 6 servings
Prep. time: 20 minutes

2 tablespoons nondairy margarine

6 tablespoons all-purpose flour

6 cups reduced-fat soymilk

Black pepper to taste

2 cans (1 pound each) creamed corn

1 tablespoon sautéed chopped onion

A delicious soup that can be easily varied by making a simple ingredient substitution.

1. In a large saucepan, melt the margarine over low heat. Add the flour and stir until smooth. Remove the pan from the heat and add the soymilk. Return the pan to the heat and bring the mixture to a boil. Simmer, stirring slowly and constantly, for about 10 minutes. Add the pepper and stir.

2. Add the creamed corn and the onion, and continue to heat and stir as necessary. Serve hot.

NUTRITIONAL FACTS PER SERVING

Calories: 263	Protein: 7 g	Carbohydrates: 48 g
Calcium: 70 mg	Total Fat: 8 g (27% fat cals)	Saturated Fat: .5 g

---

EXCHANGES, PER SERVING: 1 Fruit; 2 Starch; 1½ Fat.

Variations

Quick Cream of Celery Soup: Instead of the corn, add 1 cup chopped celery.

NUTRITIONAL FACTS PER SERVING

Calories: 143	Protein: 4.8 g	Carbohydrates: 21 g
Calcium: 71 mg	Total Fat: 4 g (25% fat cals)	Saturated Fat: 1 g

---

EXCHANGES, PER SERVING: 1 Vegetable; 1 Starch; 1 Fat.

Quick Cream of Salmon Soup: Instead of the corn and onion, add 1 can (6½ ounces) water-packed salmon and 2 tablespoons sautéed minced onion.

NUTRITIONAL FACTS PER SERVING

Calories: 205	Protein: 12 g	Carbohydrates: 20 g
Calcium: 63 mg	Total Fat: 8 g (35% fat cals)	Saturated Fat: 1 g

---

EXCHANGES, PER SERVING: 1 Lean Meat; 1 Vegetable; 1 Starch; 1 Fat.

Quick Cream of Asparagus Soup: Instead of the corn and onion, add ¾ pound chopped cooked asparagus.

NUTRITIONAL FACTS PER SERVING

Calories: 180	Protein: 9 g	Carbohydrates: 28 g
Calcium: 105 mg	Total Fat: 4.7 g (23% fat cals)	Saturated Fat: 1 g

---

EXCHANGES, PER SERVING: 2 Vegetable; 1 Starch; 1 Fat.

Quick Cream of Spinach Soup: Instead of the corn and onion, add 10 ounces finely chopped fresh spinach.

NUTRITIONAL FACTS PER SERVING

Calories: 145	Protein: 6 g	Carbohydrates: 22 g
Calcium: 108 mg	Total Fat: 4 g (25% fat cals)	Saturated Fat: 1 g

---

EXCHANGES, PER SERVING: 1 Vegetable; 1 Starch; 1 Fat.

Making Creamy Soup Without the Cream

It's not just *possible* to make a cream soup without cream—it's easy! Just use the simple base described below, and add chopped vegetables, chicken, or seafood to taste before serving. (For some great ideas, see pages 46 to 47.) No one will believe that this delicious soup is actually cream-free!

Quick Cream Soup

1. In a large saucepan, melt the margarine over low heat. Add the flour and stir until smooth. Remove the pan from the heat and add the soymilk. Return the pan to the heat and bring the mixture to a boil. Simmer, stirring slowly and constantly, for about 10 minutes. Add the pepper and stir.

2. Add 2 to 4 cups of chopped vegetables, poultry, or fish. Continue to heat and stir as necessary. Serve hot.

Yield: 6 servings
Prep. time: 20 minutes

2 tablespoons nondairy margarine

6 tablespoons all-purpose flour

6 cups reduced-fat soymilk

Black pepper to taste

Cream of Asparagus Soup

Yield: 4 servings
Prep. time: 40 minutes

4 cups reduced-fat chicken
   bouillon

2 cups chopped fresh or
   frozen asparagus

¼ cup chopped onion

1 cup nonpasteurized plain
   yogurt

Ideal for an elegant springtime repast.

1. In a large saucepan, heat the chicken bouillon over medium heat. Add the asparagus and onion, and bring to a gentle boil. Reduce the heat and simmer until the vegetables are soft, about 10 minutes. Remove the pan from the heat and allow the mixture to cool slightly.

2. Pour the mixture into a blender in small batches and blend until smooth. Pour the mixture back into the pan, add the yogurt, and stir. Serve immediately.

NUTRITIONAL FACTS PER SERVING

Calories: 70	Protein: 6 g	Carbohydrates: 10 g
Calcium: 132 mg	Total Fat: 2 g (26% fat cals)	Saturated Fat: 1 g

EXCHANGES, PER SERVING: 2 Vegetable; ½ Fat.

Cream of Broccoli Soup

Yield: 4 servings
Prep. time: 30 minutes

½ pound fresh broccoli, cut
   into ½-inch pieces

1 tablespoon low-fat
   nondairy margarine

2 tablespoons sifted
   all-purpose flour

3 cups reduced-fat chicken
   bouillon

4 ounces fresh mushrooms,
   diced

1 small potato, diced

½ cup reduced-fat soymilk

⅛ teaspoon minced garlic

Black pepper to taste

A delicious way to include a nutritious vegetable in your diet.

1. Place ½ cup water in a vegetable steamer, and steam the broccoli until tender. Set aside the broccoli and the steamer water.

2. In a large saucepan, melt the margarine over medium heat. Add the flour and stir until smooth, about 2 to 4 minutes. Add the chicken bouillon and bring to a boil. Reduce the heat and add the mushrooms, potatoes, soymilk, garlic, and black pepper; stir. Simmer until the vegetables are tender, about 10 to 15 minutes.

3. Add the steamed broccoli and the steamer water to the soup, and serve hot.

NUTRITIONAL FACTS PER SERVING

Calories: 120	Protein: 6.7 g	Carbohydrates: 15 g
Calcium: 106 mg	Total Fat: 4 g (30% fat cals)	Saturated Fat: 1.5 g

EXCHANGES, PER SERVING: 2 Vegetable; 1 Fat.

Cream of Carrot Soup

A truly elegant soup for company.

Yield: 6 servings
Prep. time: 30 minutes

1. In a large saucepan, melt the margarine over low heat. Add the carrots and onions, cover, and cook for 5 minutes. Add the chicken bouillon, potatoes, dillweed, and black pepper. Increase the heat and bring the mixture to a boil. Cover, reduce the heat, and simmer until the vegetables are tender, about 15 minutes.

2. Pour the mixture into a blender in small batches and purée. Pour back into the saucepan, add the soymilk and parsley, and heat. Serve immediately.

2 tablespoons nondairy margarine

2½ cups diced carrot

½ cup chopped onion

4 cups reduced-fat chicken bouillon

2 cups diced raw potato

½ teaspoon chopped dried dillweed

Black pepper to taste

¾ cup soymilk

¼ cup chopped fresh parsley

NUTRITIONAL FACTS PER SERVING

Calories: 148	Protein: 4 g	Carbohydrates: 23 g
Calcium: 41 mg	Total Fat: 5 g (30% fat cals)	Saturated Fat: 1 g

EXCHANGES, PER SERVING: 1½ Starch; 1 Fat.

Cucumber Spinach Soup

An unusual blend of vegetables gives this soup its unique flavor.

Yield: 6 servings
Prep. time: 50 minutes

1. In a large saucepan, combine the bouillon, cucumbers, onions, and garlic. Bring to a boil over medium heat, then lower the heat and simmer until the vegetables are soft, about 20 minutes.

2. Add the chopped spinach and simmer 5 minutes more. Allow the mixture to cool slightly.

3. Pour the mixture into a blender in small batches and purée. Transfer to a serving bowl, add the yogurt, and stir well. Cover and place in the refrigerator for at least 1 hour. Serve chilled.

3 cups reduced-fat chicken bouillon

2 cups chopped seeded peeled cucumber

1 onion, chopped

1 clove garlic, minced

1 cup chopped fresh spinach

1 cup nonpasteurized plain yogurt

NUTRITIONAL FACTS PER SERVING

Calories: 48	Protein: 3 g	Carbohydrates: 6 g
Calcium: 92 mg	Total Fat: 1 g (19% fat cals)	Saturated Fat: 0.5 g

EXCHANGES, PER SERVING: 1 Vegetable.

Cream of Tomato Soup

Yield: 4 servings
Prep. time: 15 minutes

2 cups tomato juice

2 cups soymilk

1 tablespoon nondairy
    margarine

1 tablespoon lemon juice

1/2 teaspoon dried basil

Black pepper to taste

1/4 cup cornstarch

1/2 teaspoon chopped fresh
    parsley, as garnish

An all-time favorite served with sandwiches for a quick, wholesome meal.

1. In a large saucepan, combine the tomato juice, soymilk, margarine, lemon juice, basil, and black pepper. Heat over low heat until smooth, stirring constantly.

2. When the margarine has melted, stir in the cornstarch. Heat and stir for 5 minutes more.

3. Garnish with the parsley and serve hot.

NUTRITIONAL FACTS PER SERVING

Calories: 130   Protein: 5 g   Carbohydrates: 17 g
Calcium: 33 mg   Total Fat: 3.7 g (26% fat cals) Saturated Fat: 0.3 g

---

EXCHANGES, PER SERVING: 1 Starch; 1/2 Vegetable; 1 Fat.

Tomato Bisque

Yield: 4 servings
Prep. time: 35 minutes

1 tablespoon oil

2 medium onions, thinly
    sliced

1/2 teaspoon crushed garlic

1 tablespoon cornstarch

2 cups cold water

2 pounds tomatoes,
    chopped

6 ounces soft tofu, drained
    and cut into 1-inch cubes

1 stalk celery, chopped

1 teaspoon chopped fresh
    parsley, as garnish

A colorful start for a fish meal.

1. In a large saucepan, heat the oil over medium heat. Add the onion and garlic, and sauté until browned. In a small bowl, dissolve the cornstarch in 1 cup of the water; pour into the pan and stir. Bring the mixture to a boil, stirring occasionally. Then reduce the heat and simmer for 5 minutes.

2. In a blender, purée the tomatoes. Leaving the blender running, add the tofu cubes 1 by 1. With the blender still running, slowly add the onion mixture. Blend the mixture until very smooth, then return it to the pan.

3. Add the celery and the remaining water. Heat gently for 5 minutes. Garnish with the parsley and serve hot.

NUTRITIONAL FACTS PER SERVING

Calories: 103   Protein: 5 g   Carbohydrates: 10 g
Calcium: 71 mg   Total Fat: 5 g (44% fat cals)   Saturated Fat: 3 g

---

EXCHANGES, PER SERVING: 1 1/2 Vegetable; 1 Fat.

Vichyssoise

One of the most popular cold soups. And this recipe ranks among the best!

1. In a large skillet, heat the margarine over medium heat. Add the onion and sauté until browned. Add the bouillon, potatoes, and white pepper. Bring to a boil, then cover, reduce the heat, and simmer for 25 minutes. Cool slightly.

2. Pour the mixture into a blender in small batches and blend thoroughly. Pour into a serving bowl and place in the refrigerator for at least 1 hour.

3. Serve chilled, garnished with the chopped green onion.

Yield: 6 servings
Prep. time: 1 hour

1 teaspoon nondairy margarine

1 medium onion, minced

3 cups reduced-fat chicken bouillon

3 medium potatoes, peeled and diced

White pepper to taste

1 teaspoon chopped green onion, as garnish

NUTRITIONAL FACTS PER SERVING

Calories: 60	Protein: 2 g	Carbohydrates: 8 g
Calcium: 22 mg	Total Fat: 2.7 g (40% fat cals)	Saturated Fat: 0.6 g

EXCHANGES, PER SERVING: $\frac{1}{2}$ Starch; $\frac{1}{2}$ Fat.

Cream of Zucchini Soup

Curry powder gives this aromatic soup a special flavor.

1. In a large saucepan, combine the zucchini, bouillon, onion, curry powder, and garlic. Bring to a boil over medium heat, then reduce the heat, cover, and simmer until the vegetables are tender, about 10 minutes. Cool slightly.

2. In a blender, blend the cooled mixture until smooth. Add the yogurt or sour cream and the lemon juice; blend. Transfer to a serving bowl and place in the refrigerator for at least 1 hour. Serve well chilled.

Yield: 4 servings
Prep. time: 35 minutes

3 cups sliced zucchini

2 cups reduced-fat chicken bouillon

2 medium onions, chopped

$\frac{1}{2}$ teaspoon curry powder

1 clove garlic, minced

$\frac{1}{2}$ cup nonpasteurized low-fat plain yogurt or nondairy sour cream

2 teaspoons lemon juice

NUTRITIONAL FACTS PER SERVING

Calories: 79	Protein: 6 g	Carbohydrates: 12 g
Calcium: 136 mg	Total Fat: 1.6 g (18% fat cals)	Saturated Fat: 0.8 g

EXCHANGES, PER SERVING: 2 Vegetable.

Bean and Pasta Soup

Yield: 6 servings
Prep. time: 45 minutes

2 tablespoons olive oil

¾ cup chopped green
   pepper

¾ cup finely sliced carrot

¾ cup chopped onion

¼ cup chopped celery

½ teaspoon crushed garlic

4 cups beef bouillon

3 cups water

4 medium tomatoes, peeled
   and chopped

½ teaspoon dried oregano

Black pepper to taste

2 cups macaroni, cooked
   according to package
   directions and drained

10-ounce can kidney beans

A modified, full-bodied version of the classic pasta fagioli—delicious and wholesome!

1. In a large saucepan, heat the olive oil over medium heat. Add the green pepper, carrots, onion, celery, and garlic. Sauté for 10 to 12 minutes.

2. Add the bouillon, water, tomatoes, oregano, and black pepper. Simmer for 15 minutes more.

3. Add the macaroni and kidney beans. Simmer for an additional 10 minutes. Serve hot.

NUTRITIONAL FACTS PER SERVING

Calories: 246	Protein: 8.7 g	Carbohydrates: 40 g
Calcium: 31.5 mg	Total Fat: 6 g (22% fat cals)	Saturated Fat: 1 g

EXCHANGES, PER SERVING: 2 Starch; 2 Vegetable; 1 Fat.

Clam Chowder

An easy-to-make seafood favorite. This one is a bit different from the conventional chowder.

Yield: 6 servings
Prep. time: 45 minutes

1. In a large saucepan, combine the bouillon and potatoes. Bring to a boil over medium heat, then cover, reduce the heat, and simmer for 25 minutes.

2. Pour the mixture into a blender in small batches and liquify. Return to the saucepan and add the clams and clam juice. Heat just to boiling over medium heat, then remove from the heat. Serve hot.

2 cups chicken bouillon

2 cups diced raw potato

2 cups canned minced clams

½ cup clam juice

NUTRITIONAL FACTS PER SERVING

Calories: 165	Protein: 16 g	Carbohydrates: 15 g
Calcium: 76 mg	Total Fat: 4.5 g (25% fat cals)	Saturated Fat: 1 g

EXCHANGES, PER SERVING: 2 Meat; 1 Starch.

Fish Chowder

An excellent and robust main dish, especially when served with crusty bread.

Yield: 6 servings
Prep. time: 1 hour 10 min.

1. In a large skillet, heat the oil over medium heat. Add the onion, green pepper, and garlic, and sauté until browned. Add the tomatoes, wine, water, lemon juice, and thyme. Bring to a boil, then reduce the heat and simmer for 30 minutes.

2. Add the potatoes and simmer for 15 minutes more.

3. Add the fish and simmer just until it flakes, about 2 to 3 minutes. Serve hot.

1 teaspoon oil

1 onion, chopped

1 green pepper, chopped

1 clove garlic, minced

4 cups stewed tomatoes

2 cups dry white wine

2 cups water

2 tablespoons lemon juice

½ teaspoon dried thyme

2 potatoes, peeled and diced

2 pounds red snapper or haddock, cut into 1-inch cubes

NUTRITIONAL FACTS PER SERVING

Calories: 205	Protein: 35 g	Carbohydrates: 13 g
Calcium: 111 mg	Total Fat: 6 g (26% fat cals)	Saturated Fat: 0.8 g

EXCHANGES, PER SERVING: 4 Lean Meat; ½ Starch; 1 Vegetable.

Chilled Fruit Soup

Yield: 4 servings
Prep. time: 30 minutes

1-pound can pitted dark
   cherries or 1½ cups
   frozen raspberries,
   undrained

2 tablespoons sugar

2 teaspoons lemon juice

¼ teaspoon cinnamon

4 ounces soft tofu, drained

½ cup grape juice

¼ cup red wine

4 thin lemon slices, as
   garnish

A light and flavorful summer soup for special occasions.

1. In a large saucepan, combine the cherries or raspberries with the sugar, lemon juice, and cinnamon. Bring to a boil over high heat, then reduce the heat and simmer for 5 minutes. Cool slightly.

2. Pour the mixture into a blender in small batches and purée. Filter through coarse cheesecloth and return to the blender. Add the tofu, grape juice, and wine, and blend once more. Transfer to a serving bowl and place in the refrigerator for at least 1 hour.

3. Serve well chilled, garnished with the lemon slices.

NUTRITIONAL FACTS PER SERVING

Calories: 140	Protein: 2.5 g	Carbohydrates: 23 g
Calcium: 42 mg	Total Fat: 1.2 g (8% fat cals)	Saturated Fat: 0.3 g

---

EXCHANGES, PER SERVING: 1½ Fruit.

Apricot Soup

Yield: 6 servings
Prep. time: 40 minutes

2 cups dried apricots

4¼ cups water

1 cup reduced-fat soymilk

2 tablespoons sugar

1 teaspoon lemon juice

¼ teaspoon cinnamon

6 thin lemon slices, as
   garnish

A cool, sweet soup with a different taste. It is ideal for that special meal.

1. In a large saucepan, place the apricots in 3 cups of the water. Cover and bring to a boil over medium heat, then reduce the heat and simmer for 30 minutes.

2. Pour the mixture into a blender in small batches and purée. Return to the saucepan and add the remaining water, soymilk, sugar, lemon juice, and cinnamon. Heat the soup (but do not boil) and serve hot, or place in the refrigerator for at least 1 hour and serve chilled. Garnish with the lemon slices.

NUTRITIONAL FACTS PER SERVING

Calories: 44	Protein: 1.6 g	Carbohydrates: 11 g
Calcium: 14 mg	Total Fat: 0.4 g (8% fat cals)	Saturated Fat: 0 g

---

EXCHANGES, PER SERVING: ½ Vegetable; ½ Fruit.

5

Dips

Quick and easy to make, dips are the most popular hors d'oeuvre
for entertaining. There is no limit to the ingredients
that can be used to make a dip–
or to the foods with which dips can be served.

Most conventional dips contain cream, sour cream, or cheese.
The dips in this chapter, though, are based on vegetable or soy products.
Try them as an introduction both to some important lactose-free foods
and to the use of vegetable purées to make "creamy" dishes.

Eggplant Dip

Yield: 3 cups
Prep. time: 30 minutes
Cooling time: 1 hour

1 large eggplant

¼ cup olive oil

1 teaspoon minced garlic

1½ cups diced peeled
tomato, drained

¼ cup finely chopped onion

2 tablespoons lemon juice

2 tablespoons tomato paste

Black pepper to taste

A common Mideastern delicacy, "scooped up" with triangles of pita bread. It is new to many Americans, but everyone who tries it enjoys it!

1. Peel the eggplant and cut into ½-inch cubes.

2. In a small skillet, heat the olive oil. Add the eggplant and the garlic; sauté, stirring occasionally, until the eggplant is soft enough to mash with a spoon. Transfer the eggplant to a large bowl and allow to cool for about 1 hour.

3. When cool, mash the eggplant. Add the tomato, onion, lemon juice, tomato paste, and black pepper; stir.

4. Serve at room temperature with pita bread cut in triangles.

NUTRITIONAL FACTS (PER TABLESPOON)

Calories: 13	Protein: 0.1 g	Carbohydrates: 2 g
Calcium: 1 mg	Total Fat: 1 g (69% fat cals)	Saturated Fat: 0.2 g

EXCHANGES, PER TABLESPOON: Free.

Guacamole Dip

Yield: 2 cups
Prep. time: 15 minutes
Cooling time: 1 hour

1 large tomato, peeled and
finely chopped

2 tablespoons minced onion

2 tablespoons lemon juice

1 teaspoon minced green
chili pepper

¼ teaspoon chopped garlic

2 large ripe avocados

A spicy dish common in Mexico and the southwestern United States. The word avocado comes from the ancient Aztecs.

1. In a medium bowl, combine the tomato, onion, lemon juice, green chili pepper, and garlic. Cover and place in the refrigerator for at least 1 hour.

2. In a separate bowl, mash the avocados. Add to the chilled tomato mixture; stir.

3. Serve at room temperature as a dip with raw vegetables or baked corn chips, or as a sauce with fish.

NUTRITIONAL FACTS (PER TABLESPOON)

Calories: 22	Protein: 0.3 g	Carbohydrates: 2 g
Calcium: 2 mg	Total Fat: 2 g (81% fat cals)	Saturated Fat: 0.3 g

EXCHANGES, PER TABLESPOON: ½ Fat.

Onion Dip

A tangy appetizer made without sour cream. It can be served with just about any vegetable.

Yield: 3 cups
Prep. time: 15 minutes
Cooling time: 1 hour

1. In a blender, combine the olive oil, water, lemon juice, and wine vinegar. Leaving the blender running, add the tofu cubes 1 by 1, blending until the mixture is smooth. Transfer to a large bowl.

2. Add the onion soup mix; stir well. Cover and place in the refrigerator for at least 1 hour.

3. Serve chilled with celery and carrot sticks.

½ cup olive oil

½ cup water

3 tablespoons lemon juice

1 tablespoon wine vinegar

1¾ pounds soft tofu, drained and cut into 1-inch cubes

1 envelope dehydrated onion soup mix

NUTRITIONAL FACTS (PER TABLESPOON)

Calories: 27	Protein: 1 g	Carbohydrates: 0.3 g
Calcium: 10 mg	Total Fat: 3 g (99% fat cals)	Saturated Fat: 0.2 g

EXCHANGES, PER TABLESPOON: ½ Fat.

Curry Dip

A spicy treat that depends on curry powder—a blend of many spices.

Yield: 2 cups
Prep. time: 15 minutes

1. In a blender, combine the olive oil, lemon juice, Worcestershire sauce, curry powder, dry mustard, and garlic. Leaving the blender running, add the tofu cubes 1 by 1, blending until the mixture is smooth. Transfer to a medium serving bowl.

2. Serve at room temperature with toast points.

¼ cup olive oil

2 tablespoons lemon juice

½ teaspoon Worcestershire sauce

½ teaspoon curry powder

½ teaspoon dry mustard

¼ teaspoon crushed garlic

12 ounces soft tofu, drained and cut into 1-inch cubes

NUTRITIONAL FACTS (PER TABLESPOON)

Calories: 22	Protein: 1 g	Carbohydrates: 0.3 g
Calcium: 13 mg	Total Fat: 2 g (81% fat cals)	Saturated Fat: 0.3 g

EXCHANGES, PER TABLESPOON: ½ Fat.

Hummus

Yield: 2 cups
Prep. time: 10 minutes

2 cups canned garbanzo
   beans, liquid drained and
   reserved

3 tablespoons tahini
   (sesame seed paste)

2 teaspoons lemon juice

½ teaspoon garlic powder

Pepper to taste

¼ teaspoon paprika, as
   garnish

A tantalizing Mideastern dip, this is usually served with pita bread for scooping.

1. In a blender or food processor, combine the garbanzo beans, tahini, lemon juice, garlic powder, and pepper. Add 2 tablespoons of the reserved liquid from the beans, and blend until smooth. If necessary, add 1 or 2 more tablespoons of the reserved liquid so that a creamy consistency is obtained.

2. Arrange in a flat dish, garnish with the paprika, and serve at room temperature with pita bread.

NUTRITIONAL FACTS PER SERVING (¼ CUP)

Calories: 83	Protein: 5 g	Carbohydrates: 7.5 g
Calcium: 33 mg	Total Fat: 2.7 g (29% fat cals)	Saturated Fat: 0.4 g

EXCHANGES, PER SERVING (¼ CUP): ½ Very Lean Meat; ½ Starch; ½ Fat.

Bean Dip

Yield: 2 cups
Prep. time: 15 minutes

1½ cups cooked black or
   red beans

8 ounces soft tofu, drained
   and cut into 1-inch cubes

3 tablespoons lemon juice

2 tablespoons olive oil

½ teaspoon crushed garlic

Fresh parsley sprigs, as
   garnish

A high-protein appetizer that can also be served with cold pasta as a main dish.

1. In a blender or food processor, combine the beans, tofu, lemon juice, olive oil, and garlic; blend until creamy. Transfer to a medium serving bowl and garnish with the parsley.

2. Serve at room temperature with crisp crackers.

NUTRITIONAL FACTS (PER TABLESPOON)

Calories: 15	Protein: 1 g	Carbohydrates: 1 g
Calcium: 6 mg	Total Fat: 1 g (60% fat cals)	Saturated Fat: 0.1 g

EXCHANGES, PER TABLESPOON: Free.

Mock Cream Cheese

A great accompaniment to a vegetable salad—and a delicious introduction to the use of low-lactose cheese.

Yield: 1 cup
Prep. time: 20 minutes

1. In a blender, combine the cottage cheese and vegetable oil; blend until creamy. Transfer to a small serving bowl. If desired, stir in the green pepper and/or onion.

2. Serve at room temperature as a dip or a spread. Accompany with bagel chips.

1 cup reduced-lactose cottage cheese, drained

2 tablespoons vegetable oil

1 tablespoon finely chopped green pepper, optional

1 tablespoon chopped onion, optional

NUTRITIONAL FACTS (PER TABLESPOON)

Calories: 26	Protein: 2 g	Carbohydrates: 1 g
Calcium: 9 mg	Total Fat: 2 g (69% fat cals)	Saturated Fat: 0.4 g

EXCHANGES, PER TABLESPOON: $\frac{1}{2}$ Fat.

Smoked Salmon Dip

A perennial favorite, normally made with cream cheese or sour cream. It is also a tangy sandwich spread.

Yield: 1 cup
Prep. time: 15 minutes
Cooling time: 1 hour

1. In a blender, combine all the ingredients; blend until smooth. Transfer to a small serving bowl, cover, and place in the refrigerator for at least 1 hour.

2. Serve chilled with bagel chips or rusk.

5-ounce can smoked salmon, shredded

$\frac{1}{3}$ cup nondairy cream

Black pepper to taste

NUTRITIONAL FACTS (PER TABLESPOON)

Calories: 42	Protein: 5 g	Carbohydrates: 1 g
Calcium: 21 mg	Total Fat: 2 g (43% fat cals)	Saturated Fat: 0.3 g

EXCHANGES, PER TABLESPOON: $\frac{1}{2}$ Lean Meat.

6

Sauces and Dressings

Sauces and dressings improve the taste and eye appeal of many dishes.
And with small changes in ingredients, countless variations are possible.
In fact, some two hundred different sauces are available
to the adventurous cook. While this chapter includes many basic sauces,
like Brown Sauce and Hunter's Sauce, it also presents
some more unusual creations, like exotic Peanut Sauce.
There is even a dairy-free Chocolate Sauce for those special desserts!

Mock Mayonnaise

Yield: 1¹/₂ cups
Prep. time: 2 minutes

1 cup reduced-fat soymilk

¹/₂ cup olive oil

2 teaspoons vinegar

1 teaspoon honey

¹/₄ teaspoon dry mustard

A tangy version of a favorite salad and sandwich dressing.

1. Pour the soymilk into a blender. With the blender running at low speed, slowly add the olive oil, vinegar, honey, and dry mustard. Blend until the mixture is creamy.

2. Transfer the mixture to a container with a tight-fitting lid and store in the refrigerator until needed.

NUTRITIONAL FACTS PER TABLESPOON

Calories: 43	Protein: 0.2 g	Carbohydrates: 0.8 g
Calcium: 5 mg	Total Fat: 4.6 g (96% fat cals)	Saturated Fat: 0.6 g

EXCHANGES, PER TABLESPOON: 1 Fat.

Mock Sour Cream

Yield: 1 cup
Prep. time: 2 minutes

8-ounce container reduced-lactose cottage cheese

1 tablespoon cider vinegar

1 teaspoon nondairy cream

Useful in many recipes. For cooked dishes, add it at the end of the cooking time.

1. In a blender, combine all the ingredients. Blend until the mixture has the consistency of sour cream.

2. Transfer the mixture to a container with a tight-fitting lid and store in the refrigerator until needed.

NUTRITIONAL FACTS PER TABLESPOON

Calories: 18	Protein: 3 g	Carbohydrates: 0.3 g
Calcium: 14 mg	Total Fat: 0.3 g (15% fat cals)	Saturated Fat: 0.2 g

EXCHANGES, PER TABLESPOON: Free.

Mock Sour Cream With a Twist

A useful alternative for a popular ingredient in many favorite recipes. This version is excellent over vegetables or potatoes.

1. In a small bowl, combine all the ingredients. Stir gently with a spoon until the mixture is completely smooth and creamy.

2. Transfer the mixture to a container with a tight-fitting lid and store in the refrigerator until needed.

Yield: 1 cup
Prep. time: 2 minutes

1 cup nonpasteurized plain yogurt

1 teaspoon lemon juice

1 teaspoon olive oil

NUTRITIONAL FACTS PER TABLESPOON

Calories: 11	Protein: 0.8 g	Carbohydrates: 1 g
Calcium: 25 mg	Total Fat: 0.5 g (41% fat cals)	Saturated Fat: 0.2 g

EXCHANGES, PER TABLESPOON: Free.

Variation

Stir in $\frac{1}{4}$ cup chopped chives.

Mock Cottage Cheese

A good source of protein as well as a good substitute for the real thing.

1. In a medium bowl, mash the tofu with a fork until it has the consistency of cottage cheese. Add the oil and black pepper, and stir.

2. Serve the mixture over hot cooked noodles or use in lasagna.

Yield: 2 cups
Prep. time: 5 minutes

1 pound firm tofu, drained

2 tablespoons oil

Black pepper to taste

NUTRITIONAL FACTS PER SERVING ($\frac{1}{3}$ CUP)

Calories: 88	Protein: 5.2 g	Carbohydrates: 1.6 g
Calcium: 87 mg	Total Fat: 7 g (72% fat cals)	Saturated Fat: 1 g

EXCHANGES, PER SERVING ($\frac{1}{3}$ CUP): 1 Medium Fat Meat; 1 Fat.

Variation

Substitute cinnamon for the black pepper.

Tofu Sandwich Dressing

Yield: 1 cup
Prep. time: 2 minutes

A creamy, flavorful alternative to mayonnaise that is especially good on meat and fish sandwiches.

8 ounces soft tofu, drained

1 tablespoon oil

2 tablespoons lemon juice

2 tablespoons finely
  chopped dill pickle

2 tablespoons water

1. In a blender, combine all the ingredients. Blend at medium speed until the mixture is smooth and creamy.

2. Transfer the mixture to a container with a tight-fitting lid and store in the refrigerator until needed.

NUTRITIONAL FACTS PER TABLESPOON

Calories: 10	Protein: 0.3 g	Carbohydrates: 0.1 g
Calcium: 4 mg	Total Fat: 0.9 g (90% fat cals)	Saturated Fat: 0.1 g

EXCHANGES, PER TABLESPOON: Free.

Mock Yogurt With Fruit

A delightful summertime dessert.

1. Drain the pineapple chunks, reserving 2 tablespoons of the syrup.

2. In a blender, combine the pineapple chunks, reserved pineapple syrup, tofu, and vanilla extract. Blend until the mixture has the consistency of yogurt, about 15 to 30 seconds.

3. Transfer the mixture to a container with a tight-fitting lid and store in the refrigerator until needed. Eat as is or serve over fruit.

Yield: 2 cups
Prep. time: 5 minutes

10-ounce can sweetened pineapple chunks, undrained

5 ounces soft tofu, drained and cut into 1-inch cubes

1 teaspoon vanilla extract

NUTRITIONAL FACTS PER TABLESPOON

Calories: 12	Protein: 0.5 g	Carbohydrates: 2 g
Calcium: 9 mg	Total Fat: 0.3 g (23% fat cals)	Saturated Fat: 0.1 g

EXCHANGES, PER TABLESPOON: Free.

Variations

Substitute 10 ounces frozen raspberries or strawberries, undrained, for the pineapple. Or, substitute 2 medium bananas, mashed, and 1½ cups orange juice for the pineapple.

Brown Sauce

Yield: 2 cups
Prep. time: 10 minutes

2 tablespoons nondairy
   margarine

3 tablespoons all-purpose
   flour

2 cups beef bouillon

Black pepper to taste

A classic brown sauce for beef.

1. In a medium saucepan, melt the margarine over low heat. Add the flour and cook for 2 minutes, stirring constantly. Gradually add the bouillon and cook until the mixture is smooth and slightly thickened. Season to taste with the black pepper.

2. Serve the sauce hot over beef or mashed potatoes.

NUTRITIONAL FACTS PER TABLESPOON

Calories: 10	Protein: 0.2 g	Carbohydrates: 0.7 g
Calcium: 0.7 mg	Total Fat: 0.8 g (72% fat cals)	Saturated Fat: 0.2 g

---

EXCHANGES, PER TABLESPOON: Free.

Variations

Add 2 tablespoons prepared mustard along with the black pepper. Or add ¼ cup sautéed chopped mushrooms or 2 tablespoons sautéed minced onions after adding the black pepper.

Cooking With Nondairy and Reduced-Lactose Products

Nondairy and reduced-lactose products will allow you to enjoy many of your favorite dishes *without* worrying about the discomforts of lactose intolerance. Some of these products, though, do behave differently from their lactose-containing counterparts. Here are a few hints that will help guarantee success when you cook.

• Dairy-free margarine may brown at high temperatures, so when recipes call for sautéing, heat the margarine just to melting, and then add the foods to be sautéed. Do not heat excessively.

• Nondairy cheeses and sour creams may change texture when heated to high temperatures, so add them at the *end* of the cooking time.

• Enzyme-treated milk may be sweeter than regular milk. Be sure to adjust for this by modifying the amount of sugar in your favorite dessert recipes.

• Nonpasteurized milk-based yogurt is often tolerated well by lactose-sensitive individuals, and so is a useful ingredient when cooking reduced-lactose meals. When adding yogurt to a hot dish like Beef Stroganoff, stir it in at the end of the cooking time, or add it as a garnish at the last minute. *Do not cook the yogurt,* since excessive exposure to heat causes yogurt to curdle and lose its consistency.

Sauce Stroganoff

A wonderful sauce for meat dishes that makes any recipe special.

Yield: 2 cups
Prep. time: 10 minutes

1. In a large saucepan, combine the beef bouillon with the flour over low heat; blend well. Add the tomato sauce and Worcestershire sauce, and cook until the mixture is smooth and thick, stirring constantly to prevent lumps. Remove the pan from the heat and add the mayonnaise and paprika; stir well. Set aside until ready to use.

2. When ready for the sauce, heat slowly over low heat. Add the sour cream and stir. Serve hot over braised beef, broiled lamb chops, or grilled or stewed chicken.

3. Store leftover sauce in the refrigerator.

2 cups beef bouillon

2 tablespoons all-purpose flour

¼ cup tomato sauce

1½ teaspoons Worcestershire sauce

2 tablespoons reduced-fat mayonnaise

¼ teaspoon paprika

½ cup nondairy sour cream

NUTRITIONAL FACTS PER ¼ CUP

Calories: 35	Protein: 1.4 g	Carbohydrates: 3.3 g
Calcium: 28 mg	Total Fat: 1.5 g (39% fat cals)	Saturated Fat: 0.4 g

EXCHANGES, PER ¼ CUP: Free.

Peanut Sauce

Adapted from Far Eastern cuisine, this sauce makes any meal an exotic treat.

Yield: ½ cup
Prep. time: 10 minutes

1. In a small skillet, combine the soy sauce, sesame oil, wine vinegar, oil, honey, chili oil, and garlic; heat over low heat, stirring constantly. Add the peanut butter and continue stirring until the mixture is well blended.

2. Serve the sauce warm over hot chicken or turkey, or chill and serve cold over chilled pasta.

2 tablespoons soy sauce

1 tablespoon sesame oil

1 tablespoon wine vinegar

1 tablespoon oil

1 teaspoon honey

½ teaspoon chili oil

½ teaspoon minced garlic

1 tablespoon creamy peanut butter

NUTRITIONAL FACTS PER TABLESPOON

Calories: 45	Protein: 0.9 g	Carbohydrates: 1.8 g
Calcium: 2.8 mg	Total Fat: 4 g (80% fat cals)	Saturated Fat: 0.7 g

EXCHANGES, PER TABLESPOON: 1 Fat.

White Sauce

Yield: 1 cup
Prep. time: 10 minutes

1 tablespoon nondairy
   margarine

¾ teaspoon all-purpose
   flour

1 cup soymilk

¼ teaspoon crushed garlic

A basic white sauce that should be in the repertoire of any cook.

1. In a small saucepan, combine the margarine and flour; heat over low heat for 3 minutes, stirring constantly. Gradually add the soymilk, continuing to stir. Add the garlic. Simmer the mixture for 5 minutes, still stirring.

2. Serve the sauce hot over vegetables or seafood.

NUTRITIONAL FACTS PER TABLESPOON

Calories: 30	Protein: 3 g	Carbohydrates: 2 g
Calcium: 75 mg	Total Fat: 1.6 g (48% fat cals)	Saturated Fat: 0.4 g

---

EXCHANGES, PER TABLESPOON: Free.

Variations

Sauce Florentine: Add 1 cup finely chopped spinach to the finished sauce and simmer for an additional 2 to 3 minutes. Serve hot over eggs or fish.

Sauce Italian: Add ½ tablespoon olive oil, ½ teaspoon finely chopped red or green pepper, and ½ teaspoon dried oregano to the finished sauce and simmer for an additional 5 minutes. Serve hot over salad.

Quick White Sauce

A white sauce that is easily modified with the addition of simple ingredients. Particularly good over fish, it is delicious over many other foods, as well.

1. In a small saucepan, combine the margarine and flour; stir over low heat until smooth. Add the soymilk a little at a time, still stirring. Bring the mixture to a boil, stirring constantly. Cook for 1 to 2 minutes. Add the black pepper and, if desired, the wine.

2. Serve the sauce hot over fish.

Yield: 1 cup
Prep. time: 10 minutes

2 tablespoons nondairy margarine

2 tablespoons all-purpose flour

1 cup reduced-fat soymilk

Black pepper to taste

1 tablespoon white wine, optional

NUTRITIONAL FACTS PER TABLESPOON

Calories: 20	Protein: 0.6 g	Carbohydrates: 0.8 g
Calcium: 19 mg	Total Fat: 1.7 g (77% fat cals)	Saturated Fat: 0.3 g

EXCHANGES, PER TABLESPOON: Free.

Variations

Anchovy Sauce: Add 1 teaspoon chopped canned anchovies to the finished sauce.

Cheese Sauce: Add 1 tablespoon grated hard cheese (Swiss, Parmesan, or Cheddar), if tolerated, to the finished sauce.

Egg Sauce: Add 1 hard-cooked egg, finely chopped, to the finished sauce.

Horseradish Sauce: Add 1 tablespoon grated fresh horseradish to the finished sauce.

Lime Sauce: Add 1 tablespoon lime juice to the finished sauce.

Mustard Sauce: Add 1 teaspoon dry mustard to the finished sauce.

Shrimp Sauce: Add 2 tablespoons finely chopped cooked shrimp to the finished sauce.

Turmeric Sauce: Add 1 tablespoon turmeric powder to the finished sauce.

Sherried White Sauce

Yield: 1 cup
Prep. time: 10 minutes

2 tablespoons nondairy margarine

2 tablespoons all-purpose flour

1 cup reduced-lactose skim milk

2 tablespoons chopped chives

1 teaspoon dry sherry

Black pepper to taste

Versatile, basic, and flavorful.

1. In a small saucepan, melt the margarine over low heat. Remove the pan from the heat and add the flour; stir until smooth. Return the pan to the heat and gradually add the milk, stirring constantly. Stir until the mixture has thickened. Add the chives, sherry, and pepper.

2. Use the sauce in a soufflé or serve it hot over fish, chicken, poached eggs, or vegetables, especially asparagus.

NUTRITIONAL FACTS PER TABLESPOON

Calories: 21	Protein: 0.6 g	Carbohydrates: 1 g
Calcium: 19 mg	Total Fat: 1.8 g (77% fat cals)	Saturated Fat: 0.2 g

EXCHANGES, PER TABLESPOON: Free.

Variation

Newburg Sauce: Add 2 tablespoons shredded sautéed lobster meat to the finished sauce. Serve hot over seafood.

White Sauce With Basil

Yield: 1 cup
Prep. time: 10 minutes

3 tablespoons nondairy margarine

3 tablespoons all-purpose flour

1 cup chicken bouillon

1/8 teaspoon finely chopped onion

1/8 teaspoon dried basil

Black pepper to taste

A different kind of white sauce, made without any milk.

1. In a small saucepan, melt the margarine over low heat. Add the flour and stir until the mixture is smooth. Gradually add the bouillon, stirring constantly until the mixture has thickened. Add the onion, basil, and black pepper.

2. Serve the sauce hot over vegetables, eggs, or shredded chicken.

NUTRITIONAL FACTS PER TABLESPOON

Calories: 26	Protein: 0.4 g	Carbohydrates: 1 g
Calcium: 1.5 mg	Total Fat: 2 g (69% fat cals)	Saturated Fat: 0.4 g

EXCHANGES, PER TABLESPOON: 1/2 Fat.

Sauce à la King

Makes a lunch or dinner entrée especially attractive. Use it to enhance leftovers.

Yield: 1 cup
Prep. time: 15 minutes

1. In a medium skillet, melt the margarine over low heat. Add the mushrooms and green pepper, and sauté until soft. Add 3 to 4 tablespoons of the cream and the flour; stir until smooth. Add the remaining cream and the bouillon; stir. Add the white pepper. Heat the mixture until it has thickened; do not boil it.

2. Mix the sauce with tuna, salmon, shredded chicken, or diced meat. Season to taste and serve over toast or rice, or in crêpes.

2 tablespoons nondairy margarine

½ cup chopped fresh mushrooms

1 tablespoon chopped green pepper

½ cup nondairy cream

1½ tablespoons all-purpose flour

½ cup chicken bouillon

⅛ teaspoon white pepper

NUTRITIONAL FACTS PER TABLESPOON

Calories: 16   Protein: 1 g   Carbohydrates: 1.5 g
Calcium: 0.6 mg   Total Fat: 1.4 g (78% fat cals)   Saturated Fat: 0.1 g

EXCHANGES, PER TABLESPOON: Free.

Creamy Dill Sauce

A distinctively flavored sauce, especially good on fresh salmon.

Yield: 1 cup
Prep. time: 5 minutes

1. In a small saucepan, combine the cornstarch with a small amount of the bouillon over medium heat; stir to blend. Add the remaining bouillon and bring to boil, stirring constantly. Add the yogurt and dill, and stir.

2. Serve the sauce hot over fish, meat, or vegetables.

1 tablespoon cornstarch

1 cup chicken bouillon

½ cup nonpasteurized plain yogurt

½ teaspoon dried dill

NUTRITIONAL FACTS PER TABLESPOON

Calories: 11   Protein: 1.7 g   Carbohydrates: 1.6 g
Calcium: 13 mg   Total Fat: 0.2 g (11% fat cals)   Saturated Fat: 1.1 g

EXCHANGES, PER TABLESPOON: Free.

Hunter's Sauce

Yield: 2 cups
Prep. time: 20 minutes

3 tablespoons nondairy margarine

1 tablespoon finely chopped onion

1 cup finely chopped mushrooms

½ cup dry white wine

1 cup chicken bouillon

¼ cup tomato paste

1 teaspoon chopped fresh parsley

A traditional French sauce for meat and fowl.

1. In a medium saucepan, melt the margarine over medium heat. Add the onions and sauté until soft and transparent. Add the mushrooms and sauté for an additional 3 to 4 minutes. Add the wine and bring the mixture to a boil. Reduce the heat to low and simmer the mixture until reduced by half.

2. Add the bouillon, tomato paste, and parsley. Cook for 2 to 3 minutes more. Stir constantly.

3. Serve the sauce hot over sautéed or broiled chicken or meat.

NUTRITIONAL FACTS PER TABLESPOON

Calories: 16	Protein: 0.1 g	Carbohydrates: 0.9 g
Calcium: 1 mg	Total Fat: 1 g (56% fat cals)	Saturated Fat: 0.2 g

EXCHANGES, PER TABLESPOON: Free.

Pesto Sauce

Yield: 1 cup
Prep time: 2 minutes

¾ cup tightly packed fresh basil

¾ cup tightly packed fresh spinach

½ cup chicken broth

1 tablespoon plus 1 teaspoon extra virgin olive oil

3–4 cloves garlic, peeled

2 teaspoons lemon juice

¼ teaspoon ground white pepper

A savory sauce for hot or chilled pasta.

1. In a blender, combine all the ingredients. Blend until the mixture is smooth.

2. Serve the sauce at room temperature over hot or chilled pasta.

NUTRITIONAL FACTS PER TABLESPOON

Calories: 22	Protein: .2 g	Carbohydrates: 2.4 g
Calcium: 70 mg	Total Fat: 1.3 g (53% fat cals)	Saturated Fat: 0 g

EXCHANGES, PER TABLESPOON: Free.

Egg-Free Hollandaise Sauce

A butter- and egg-free version of the classic sauce commonly served over asparagus.

Yield: 1 cup
Prep. time: 10 minutes

1. In a small bowl, combine the water and cornstarch; stir until the cornstarch is dissolved. In a small saucepan, combine the cornstarch mixture with the soymilk and oil over medium heat. Bring to a boil, reduce the heat to low, and simmer the mixture until thickened, about 5 minutes, stirring constantly. Add the lemon juice.

2. Serve the sauce hot over vegetables. Garnish with the paprika.

2 tablespoons water

1 tablespoon cornstarch

1 cup reduced-fat soymilk

1 tablespoon canola or olive oil

1 tablespoon lemon juice

Paprika, as garnish

NUTRITIONAL FACTS PER TABLESPOON

Calories: 12	Protein: 0.5 g	Carbohydrates: 0.3 g
Calcium: 4 mg	Total Fat: 1 g (75% fat cals)	Saturated Fat: 0.1 g

EXCHANGES, PER TABLESPOON: Free.

Variations

Add 3 tablespoons nondairy whipped topping, 3 tablespoons chopped fresh cucumber, or 2 tablespoons dry white wine to the finished sauce. Serve hot over vegetables or eggs.

Shopping for Lactose-Free Foods

While foods labeled "lactose-reduced" are, of course, safe for the lactose-intolerant person, there's no need to limit yourself to products that bear this label. By shopping smart, you can enjoy a wide range of foods *without* suffering the symptoms of lactose intolerance.

One great strategy is to become familiar with the ethnic foods available in supermarkets and specialty stores. For instance, many Asian, Indian, and Spanish foods are milk-free. And Jewish foods la-beled "Parve" are absolutely dairy-free. Some manufacturers identify foods containing dairy products by placing a "D" on the label. Look for this mark, and then examine the ingredients list to see if the product is appropriate for you. In fact, the ingredients list should always be checked to make sure that the product does not contain a food that is likely to cause a problem. If in doubt, most companies have hotlines that can answer your questions.

Tartar Sauce

Yield: 1 cup
Prep. time: 2 minutes

1 cup reduced-fat
  mayonnaise

½ cup chopped dill pickle

2 tablespoons cider vinegar

⅛ teaspoon onion powder

A peppy sauce for broiled or sautéed fish.

1. In a small bowl, combine all the ingredients. Stir until the mixture is well blended.

2. Transfer the mixture to a container with a tight-fitting lid and store in the refrigerator until needed.

NUTRITIONAL FACTS PER TABLESPOON

Calories: 40	Protein: 0 g	Carbohydrates: 3 g
Calcium: 0 mg	Total Fat: 3 g (67% fat cals)	Saturated Fat: 1 g

EXCHANGES, PER TABLESPOON: ½ Fat.

Horseradish Sauce

Yield: 1 cup
Prep. time: 5 minutes

1 cup reduced-fat
  mayonnaise

½ cup nonpasteurized plain
  yogurt

¼ cup drained prepared
  white horseradish

Black pepper to taste

A zippy sauce that adds tang to any kind of meat or fish.

1. In a small bowl, combine all the ingredients. Stir until the mixture is well blended.

2. Serve the sauce cold with meat or fish, especially smoked fish.

NUTRITIONAL FACTS PER TABLESPOON

Calories: 46	Protein: 0.4 g	Carbohydrates: 3.8 g
Calcium: 14 mg	Total Fat: 3 g (60% fat cals)	Saturated Fat: 1 g

EXCHANGES, PER TABLESPOON: ½ Fat.

Custard Sauce

A creamy sauce that makes any fruit dessert special.

1. In a small bowl, combine the cornstarch with $\frac{1}{4}$ cup of the cream; stir until smooth. In a medium saucepan, combine the remaining cream with the milk, sugar, vanilla extract, and orange rind; bring to a boil over medium heat, stirring constantly. Add the cornstarch mixture and stir until thoroughly blended. Reduce the heat and simmer, stirring gently, until the sauce begins to thicken.

2. Serve the sauce warm over fruit desserts.

Yield: 2 cups
Prep. time: 10 minutes

2 tablespoons cornstarch

1 cup nondairy cream

1 cup reduced-lactose skim milk

$\frac{1}{4}$ cup sugar

1 teaspoon vanilla extract

$\frac{1}{4}$ teaspoon grated orange rind

NUTRITIONAL FACTS PER TABLESPOON

Calories: 20	Protein: 0 g	Carbohydrates: 3 g
Calcium: 10 mg	Total Fat: 1 g (45% fat cals)	Saturated Fat: 0 g

EXCHANGES: Free.

Chocolate Sauce

An all-time favorite that makes dessert time party time.

1. In a blender, combine all the ingredients. Blend until the mixture is smooth.

2. Serve the sauce cold over nondairy ice cream or pudding.

Yield: 1 cup
Prep. time: 2 minutes

$\frac{1}{2}$ cup sugar

$\frac{1}{2}$ cup nondairy cream, warmed

3 tablespoons water

$\frac{1}{8}$ cup bittersweet chocolate chips

1 tablespoon rum

$\frac{1}{4}$ teaspoon vanilla extract

NUTRITIONAL FACTS PER TABLESPOON

Calories: 46	Protein: 0 g	Carbohydrates: 8 g
Calcium: 8.5 mg	Total Fat: 1.6 g (30% fat cals)	Saturated Fat: 0.8 g

EXCHANGES, PER TABLESPOON: $\frac{1}{2}$ Starch.

Fruit Topping

Yield: 1 cup
Prep. time: 10 minutes

2 tablespoons cold water

1 tablespoon cornstarch

1 cup apricot nectar

2 tablespoons sugar

Especially delicious over cooked cereal such as oatmeal.

1. In a small bowl, combine the water and cornstarch; stir until the mixture has the consistency of a smooth paste. In a small saucepan, combine the apricot nectar and sugar; heat to boiling over medium heat. Add the cornstarch mixture and stir. Reduce the heat and simmer the mixture, stirring constantly, until it is thick and clear.

2. Serve the sauce warm over pudding or hot cereal.

NUTRITIONAL FACTS PER TABLESPOON

Calories: 9	Protein: 0 g	Carbohydrates: 2 g
Calcium: 1 mg	Total Fat: 0 g (0% fat cals)	Saturated Fat: 0 g

EXCHANGES: Free.

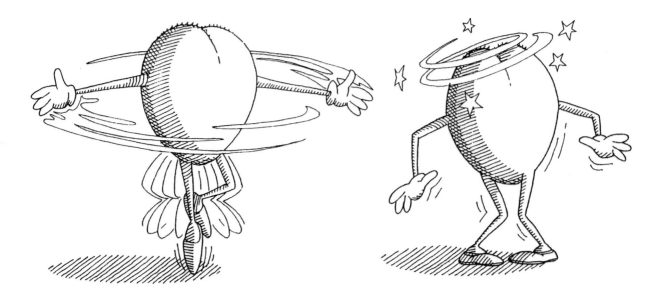

Green Goddess Dressing

A colorful garnish for fish dishes that also adds flavor.

Yield: 2 cups
Prep. time: 5 minutes

1. In a blender, combine all the ingredients. Blend until the mixture is smooth.

2. Serve the dressing with fish, shellfish, or salad.

2 cups reduced-fat
   mayonnaise

½ cup nonpasteurized plain
   yogurt

2 tablespoons chopped chives

2 tablespoons lemon juice

1 tablespoon dried parsley

1 tablespoon vinegar

½ teaspoon crushed garlic

3 anchovy fillets

NUTRITIONAL FACTS PER TABLESPOON

Calories: 43	Protein: 0.3 g	Carbohydrates: 3 g
Calcium: 7 mg	Total Fat: 3 g (63% fat cals)	Saturated Fat: 1 g

EXCHANGES, PER TABLESPOON: ½ Fat.

Herb Dressing

Wonderful over raw vegetables served either before the meal as an appetizer or with the meal as a side dish.

Yield: 1 cup
Prep. time: 5 minutes

1. In a blender, combine the parsley, lemon juice, water, olive oil, ground ginger, celery seed, garlic, and black pepper; purée until smooth. Leaving the blender running, add the tofu a little at a time. Blend until the mixture is thick and smooth, about 1 minute.

2. Serve the dressing over a mixed green salad.

¼ cup chopped fresh parsley

3 tablespoons lemon juice

2 tablespoons water

1 tablespoon olive oil

½ teaspoon ground ginger

⅛ teaspoon celery seed

1 clove garlic, minced

Black pepper to taste

½ cup soft tofu, drained and
   mashed

NUTRITIONAL FACTS PER TABLESPOON

Calories: 10	Protein: 0.3 g	Carbohydrates: 0.1 g
Calcium: 4 mg	Total Fat: 1 g (90% fat cals)	Saturated Fat: 0.2 g

EXCHANGES, PER TABLESPOON: Free.

Russian Dressing

Yield: 1 cup
Prep. time: 5 minutes

¼ cup water

3½ tablespoons tomato ketchup

2 tablespoons lemon juice

2 tablespoons olive oil

1 teaspoon Worcestershire sauce

2 ounces soft tofu

Excellent in chicken or turkey sandwiches. For elegant canapés, trim off the crusts and cut the sandwiches into triangles.

1. In a blender, combine the water, ketchup, lemon juice, olive oil, and Worcestershire sauce. Leaving the blender running, add the tofu cubes 1 by 1, blending until the mixture is creamy.

2. Serve the dressing over a mixed green salad or as part of a Monte Cristo sandwich.

NUTRITIONAL FACTS PER TABLESPOON

Calories: 20	Protein: 0.2 g	Carbohydrates: 0.9 g
Calcium: 2.7 mg	Total Fat: 1.8 g (81% fat cals)	Saturated Fat: 0.3 g

EXCHANGES, PER TABLESPOON: Free.

Lemon-Mustard Dressing

Yield: 1 cup
Prep. time: 2 minutes

¾ cup olive oil

2 teaspoons grated lemon rind

2 teaspoons dry mustard

Black pepper to taste

2 tablespoons lemon juice

Zips up the flavor of salads by adding an unusual flavor combination.

1. In a blender, combine the olive oil, lemon rind, dry mustard, and black pepper; blend well. Add the lemon juice and blend just 2 to 3 seconds more.

2. Serve the dressing over bean salad.

NUTRITIONAL FACTS PER TABLESPOON

Calories: 90	Protein: 0 g	Carbohydrates: 0 g
Calcium: 0 mg	Total Fat: 10 g (100% fat cals)	Saturated Fat: 0 g

EXCHANGES, PER TABLESPOON: 2 Fat.

Lemon Cream Dressing

An unusual but flavorful substitute for sour cream.

Yield: ½ cup
Prep. time: 5 minutes

1. In a blender, combine the soymilk, oil, lemon juice, and honey. Leaving the blender running, add the tofu gradually, blending until the mixture is smooth. Transfer the dressing to a bowl, cover, and place in the refrigerator for at least 1 hour.

2. Serve over baked potatoes or as a garnish for soup.

¼ cup soymilk

2 tablespoons oil

1 tablespoon lemon juice

½ teaspoon honey

4 ounces soft tofu

NUTRITIONAL FACTS PER TABLESPOON

Calories: 40   Protein: 1 g   Carbohydrates: 1.5 g
Calcium: 20 mg   Total Fat: 3.5 g (79% fat cals)   Saturated Fat: 0.6 g

EXCHANGES, PER TABLESPOON: ½ Fat.

Honey Lime Dressing

Lends a really unique flavor to fruit.

Yield: 1 cup
Prep. time: 2 minutes

1. In a jar with a tight-fitting lid, combine all the ingredients. Shake the jar vigorously, then place it in the refrigerator for at least 1 hour.

2. Serve the dressing well chilled over fruit such as melon chunks or peach slices.

¾ cup prepared French dressing

2 tablespoons honey

2 tablespoons lime juice

½ teaspoon chopped dried dillweed

NUTRITIONAL FACTS PER TABLESPOON

Calories: 275   Protein: 0 g   Carbohydrates: 8 g
Calcium: 1.6 mg   Total Fat: 5 g (16% fat cals)   Saturated Fat: 1 g

EXCHANGES, PER TABLESPOON: ½ Starch; 1 Fat.

7

Vegetables, Beans, and Pasta

All vegetables are cholesterol-free, with very little fat.
In addition, most are high in nutrients. Carrots, for instance,
are an excellent source of vitamin A, while leafy greens such as
collards and kale provide calcium. And, of course,
all vegetables are packed with fiber.

Beans, too, are lean and nutritious fare, with lots of protein, iron,
calcium, magnesium, and fiber. Satisfying and flavorful,
beans can be used in a refreshing salad, or as a delicious
low-fat substitute in dishes such as Mock Chopped Liver.
And when beans are combined with pasta, you have a dish that is
not only hearty, but also a complete protein–
an important consideration when consuming a milk-free diet.

Creamed Broccoli

Yield: 4 servings
Prep. time: 5 minutes
Baking time: 30 minutes

10-ounce package frozen chopped broccoli

10¾-ounce can condensed nondairy mushroom soup

¼ cup reduced-fat soymilk

¼ cup low-fat nondairy margarine

1 egg, beaten

An excellent source of vitamin A.

1. Preheat the oven to 350°F. Lightly coat a 1½-quart casserole dish with nonstick cooking spray.

2. In a medium saucepan, cook the broccoli according to package directions just until the pieces can be separated with a fork; drain. Arrange the broccoli pieces in 1 layer in the casserole dish.

3. In a blender, combine the soup, soymilk, margarine, and egg; blend until thoroughly mixed, about 1 minute. Pour the sauce over the broccoli.

4. Cover the dish, place it in the oven, and bake until thoroughly heated, about 30 minutes. Serve immediately.

NUTRITIONAL FACTS PER SERVING

Calories: 120	Protein: 5 g	Carbohydrates: 10 g
Calcium: 111 mg	Total Fat: 5 g (37% fat cals)	Saturated Fat: 1 g

EXCHANGES, PER SERVING: ½ Vegetable; ½ Starch; 1 Fat.

Creamed Artichoke Hearts

Yield: 4 servings
Prep. time: 10 minutes
Baking time: 15 minutes

1-pound can water-packed artichoke hearts, drained

¼ cup Creamy Dill Sauce (see page 71)

1 teaspoon grated onion

¼ cup dairy-free bread crumbs

An unusual way to serve artichoke hearts.

1. Preheat the oven to 350°F. Lightly coat a 1-quart casserole dish with nonstick cooking spray.

2. In the casserole dish, arrange the artichoke hearts in 1 layer.

3. In a small bowl, combine the Creamy Dill Sauce and onion; stir until blended. Pour the sauce over the artichokes and sprinkle with the bread crumbs.

4. Place the dish in the oven and bake until the artichokes are hot and the sauce is bubbling, about 15 minutes. Serve immediately.

NUTRITIONAL FACTS PER SERVING

Calories: 100	Protein: 3 g	Carbohydrates: 13 g
Calcium: 27 mg	Total Fat: 1.4 g (13% fat cals)	Saturated Fat: 0.3 g

EXCHANGES, PER SERVING: ½ Starch; 1 Vegetable.

Carrot Pudding

A colorful, sweet-tasting vegetable accompaniment for any meat or fish entrée.

1. Preheat the oven to 350°F. Lightly coat a 1½-quart casserole dish with nonstick cooking spray.

2. In a large bowl, beat the egg yolks with the sugar until light and fluffy. Gradually add the orange juice, stirring. Stir in the carrots and orange rind. In a medium bowl, beat the egg whites until stiff but not dry; fold into the carrot batter.

3. Turn the mixture into the casserole dish. Place the dish in the oven and bake until the carrots are hot, about 30 minutes. Serve immediately.

Yield: 6 servings
Prep. time: 15 minutes
Baking time: 30 minutes

3 eggs, separated

3 tablespoons sugar

¼ cup orange juice

3 cups shredded raw carrot

1 teaspoon grated orange rind

NUTRITIONAL FACTS PER SERVING

Calories: 88	Protein: 3.5 g	Carbohydrates: 12 g
Calcium: 29 mg	Total Fat: 2.8 g (28% fat cals)	Saturated Fat: 0.7 g

EXCHANGES, PER SERVING: ½ Medium Fat Meat; 1 Vegetable; ½ Starch.

Creamed Spinach

A delicious spinach dish served either as a meat or fish accompaniment or as part of a vegetable plate.

1. In a small bowl, dissolve the potato starch in the water. In a small saucepan, melt the margarine over medium heat. Add the dissolved potato starch and stir. Add the bouillon and bring the mixture to a boil. Reduce the heat and simmer, stirring constantly, until the sauce is thick and smooth. Remove from the heat and season with the black pepper.

2. In a large bowl, combine the spinach and the sauce; toss to mix well. Serve immediately.

Yield: 6 servings
Prep. time: 15 minutes

1 tablespoon potato starch

2 tablespoons cold water

1 tablespoon nondairy margarine

¾ cup chicken bouillon

Black pepper to taste

20-ounce package frozen chopped spinach, cooked according to package directions and drained

---

NUTRITIONAL FACTS PER SERVING

Calories: 50	Protein: 3.5 g	Carbohydrates: 6 g
Calcium: 118 mg	Total Fat: 2.4 g (17% fat cals)	Saturated Fat: 0.4 g

EXCHANGES, PER SERVING: 1 Vegetable; ½ Fat.

Spinach Pie With Cottage Cheese

Yield: 8 servings
Prep. time: 15 minutes
Baking time: 1 hour 10 min.

1½ cups chopped onion

20-ounce package frozen chopped spinach, thawed and drained

1 pound reduced-lactose cottage cheese or mashed soft tofu

2 eggs

½ cup egg substitute

½ cup chopped green onions

2 tablespoons dried dill

2 tablespoons dried parsley

Black pepper to taste

8-ounce package phyllo leaves

¼ cup vegetable oil

An outstanding version of a classic Greek dish. It is also wonderful served cold the next day!

1. Preheat the oven to 350°F. Lightly coat a large skillet and a 12-x-9-inch baking pan with nonstick cooking spray.

2. In the skillet, sauté the onions over medium heat until soft. Add the spinach and sauté for 3 to 4 minutes more.

3. In a large bowl, combine the cottage cheese or tofu, eggs, egg substitute, green onions, dill, parsley, and black pepper; mix well. Add the spinach and onions, and mix again.

4. Fit 12 leaves of the phyllo dough into the baking pan 1 sheet at a time, brushing each sheet very lightly with some of the vegetable oil after arranging it in the pan. Add the spinach filling, using a rubber spatula to spread it to the edges and into the corners. Top with 12 more sheets of phyllo, oiled. Using a sharp knife, score the top layer of phyllo into 8 squares.

5. Place the baking pan in the oven and bake, uncovered, until the spinach pie has browned, about 1 hour and 10 minutes. Serve hot.

NUTRITIONAL FACTS PER SERVING

Calories: 250	Protein: 16 g	Carbohydrates: 28 g
Calcium: 129 mg	Total Fat: 8.6 g (30% fat cals)	Saturated Fat: 1.5 g

---

EXCHANGES, PER SERVING: 1½ Lean Meat; 1 Vegetable; 1½ Starch; 1 Fat.

Asparagus on Toast Points

An elegant springtime accompaniment for fish entrées.

1. In a small skillet, melt the margarine over low heat. Add the asparagus and toss to coat. Cook until the asparagus are tender, about 10 minutes.

2. In a small saucepan, combine the cream and black pepper; stir over low heat for just about 15 seconds.

3. Arrange the toast on 6 individual sandwich plates, 2 halves per plate. Divide the asparagus into 6 servings and arrange on top of the toast. Pour the cream over the asparagus. Serve immediately.

Yield: 6 servings
Prep. time: 20 minutes

2 teaspoons nondairy margarine

2 pounds fresh asparagus, washed and cut into 2-inch lengths

3 tablespoons nondairy cream

Black pepper to taste

6 slices dairy-free white bread, toasted and cut in half diagonally

NUTRITIONAL FACTS PER SERVING

Calories: 105 Protein: 4 g Carbohydrates: 17 g
Calcium: 54 mg Total Fat: 3 g (26% fat cals) Saturated Fat: 0.8 g

EXCHANGES, PER SERVING: $\frac{1}{2}$ Vegetable; 1 Starch; $\frac{1}{2}$ Fat.

Baked Acorn Squash

A winter vegetable, high in vitamin A and absolutely delicious!

1. Preheat the oven to 350°F.

2. Cut the squash in half and remove the seeds. Brush the cavities with the melted margarine, then place 1 tablespoon honey in each cavity. Arrange the squash halves in a 13-x-9-inch baking pan with the cut sides up. Place the pan in the oven and bake until the squash halves are soft, about 45 minutes.

3. Remove the pan from the oven and sprinkle the squash halves with the crushed walnuts. Place the pan back in the oven for 5 minutes. Serve immediately.

Yield: 6 servings
Prep. time: 10 minutes
Baking time: 45 minutes

3 medium acorn squash

1 tablespoon low-fat nondairy margarine, melted

6 tablespoons honey

2 tablespoons crushed walnuts

NUTRITIONAL FACTS PER SERVING

Calories: 185 Protein: 2 g Carbohydrates: 34 g
Calcium: 21 mg Total Fat: 4 g (19% fat cals) Saturated Fat: 0.3 g

EXCHANGES, PER SERVING: 2 Starch; $\frac{1}{2}$ Fat.

Spaghetti Squash

Yield: 4 servings
Prep. time: 10 minutes
Baking time: 40 minutes

2 medium spaghetti squash

1 tablespoon nondairy
   margarine

8-ounce can tomato sauce

$\frac{1}{8}$ teaspoon dried oregano

A fun vegetable, high in vitamin A. It looks and tastes just like spaghetti!

1. Preheat the oven to 350°F.

2. Cut the squash in half and remove the seeds. Arrange the squash halves in a 12-x-9-inch baking pan with the cut sides up. Dot with the margarine. Place the pan in the oven and bake until the squash halves are soft, about 40 minutes. Remove from the oven and place each squash half on an individual dinner plate.

3. In a small saucepan, combine the tomato sauce and oregano. Heat over low heat until bubbly, about 5 minutes. Pour the sauce over the hot squash halves.

4. Serve immediately. Direct your guests to eat the squash by scoring the meat with a fork, causing the squash to separate into spaghetti-like strands. Eat the strands like spaghetti.

NUTRITIONAL FACTS PER SERVING

Calories: 109	Protein: 2 g	Carbohydrates: 13 g
Calcium: 33 mg	Total Fat: 5 g (41% fat cals)	Saturated Fat: 0.6 g

EXCHANGES, PER SERVING: 1 Starch; 1 Fat.

Steamed Greens

A conventional but savory way to serve leafy greens.

Yield: 3 servings
Prep. time: 35 minutes

1. Strip off the leaves from the greens and remove the tough stems; wash well.

2. Place the greens in a medium saucepan and add just enough water to barely cover them. Bring the water to a boil over medium heat, then reduce the heat and simmer until the greens are tender, at least 30 minutes.

3. Drain the greens and place in a serving bowl. Season with the black pepper and/or lemon juice.

4. Serve hot with meat or fish.

½ pound collard greens, kale, beet greens, or turnip greens

Black pepper to taste and/or 1 teaspoon lemon juice

NUTRITIONAL FACTS PER SERVING

Calories: 22   Protein: 2 g   Carbohydrates: 4 g
Calcium: 116 mg   Total Fat: 0 g (0% fat cals)   Saturated Fat: 0 g

EXCHANGES, PER SERVING: 1 Vegetable.

Collards With Onions and Ginger

Yield: 6 servings
Prep. time: 10 minutes

1 teaspoon nondairy
  margarine

¼ cup minced onion

1 pound collard greens,
  cooked (see Steamed
  Greens, page 87)

¼ cup chopped mushrooms

¼ teaspoon ground ginger

A healthy, colorful version of a side dish popular in the South.

1. In a large skillet, melt the margarine over medium heat. Add the onions and sauté until browned. Add the steamed collard greens and the mushrooms, and sauté for 3 to 4 minutes more. Remove the pan from the heat and sprinkle the vegetables with the ginger; toss to mix.

2. Serve warm with meat or fish.

NUTRITIONAL FACTS PER SERVING

Calories: 32	Protein: 2.3 g	Carbohydrates: 4.6 g
Calcium: 119 mg	Total Fat: 0.7 g (20% fat cals)	Saturated Fat: 0 g

EXCHANGES, PER SERVING: 1 Vegetable.

Sautéed Turnip Greens

Yield: 6 servings
Prep. time: 20 minutes

1 pound turnip greens

1 tablespoon nondairy
  margarine

½ teaspoon lemon juice

A legendary Southern favorite that makes an excellent side dish.

1. Strip off the leaves from the turnip greens and remove the tough stems. Wash the greens well and dry with paper toweling. Chop into ½-inch pieces.

2. In a large skillet, melt the margarine over medium heat. Add the turnip greens and sauté until tender, about 10 minutes.

3. Just before serving, add the lemon juice and toss to mix. Serve hot.

NUTRITIONAL FACTS PER SERVING

Calories: 30	Protein: 2.2 g	Carbohydrates: 4.4 g
Calcium: 118 mg	Total Fat: 0.7 g (21% fat cals)	Saturated Fat: 0 g

EXCHANGES, PER SERVING: 1 Vegetable.

Turnip Soufflé

An unusual and delicious dish that can be an accompaniment or an entrée.

1. Preheat the oven to 375°F. Lightly coat a 1½-quart casserole dish with nonstick cooking spray.

2. Peel and slice the turnips. In a medium saucepan, bring the turnips and ½ cup water to a boil over medium heat. Reduce the heat to low and simmer until the turnips are tender, about 20 minutes. Add water to the saucepan as necessary. Drain the turnips and place in the casserole dish.

3. In a medium bowl, beat the egg whites until stiff but not dry. In a small skillet, melt the margarine over low heat. Add the flour to the skillet, stirring until smooth. Add the soymilk and egg yolks, and stir. Remove the pan from the heat and fold in the egg whites. Pour the mixture over the turnips in the casserole dish and toss to mix.

4. Place the casserole dish in the oven and bake until the soufflé is set, about 40 minutes.

5. Remove the soufflé from the oven and serve immediately.

Yield: 6 servings
Prep. time: 35 minutes
Baking time: 40 minutes

6 medium turnips

2 eggs, separated

1 tablespoon low-fat nondairy margarine

2 tablespoons all-purpose flour

¼ cup reduced-fat soymilk

NUTRITIONAL FACTS PER SERVING

Calories: 55	Protein: 2.7 g	Carbohydrates: 4 g
Calcium: 28 mg	Total Fat: 2.5 g (40% fat cals)	Saturated Fat: 0.5 g

EXCHANGES, PER SERVING: 1 Vegetable; ½ Fat.

Potato Pancakes

Yield: 12 pancakes
Prep. time: 20 minutes

1 egg

¼ cup egg substitute

2 cups grated unpeeled raw
    potato

1 small onion, minced

1 tablespoon potato starch

¼ teaspoon baking powder

Garlic powder to taste

Black pepper to taste

Traditionally served at the festival of Hanukkah, but universally enjoyed! Serve with nondairy sour cream.

1. In a medium bowl, combine the egg and egg substitute; beat thoroughly with a fork. Add the potatoes and mix. Add the onion, potato starch, baking powder, garlic powder, and black pepper, and stir well.

2. Spray a griddle with nonstick cooking spray and heat over medium heat. Drop the batter by spoonfuls onto the griddle and cook until the undersides of the pancakes are golden brown, about 1 to 2 minutes. Gently turn the pancakes using a spatula and cook an additional minute. Slide the pancakes off the griddle and onto absorbent paper toweling. Blot, transfer to a plate, and cover to keep warm.

3. Serve hot with applesauce.

NUTRITIONAL FACTS PER SERVING (3 PANCAKES)

Calories: 120	Protein: 4 g	Carbohydrates: 20 g
Calcium: 41 mg	Total Fat: 2.5 g (19% fat cals)	Saturated Fat: 0 g

EXCHANGES, PER SERVING (3 PANCAKES): 1 Starch; ½ Fat.

Five Bean Salad

Yield: 6 servings
Prep. time: 10 minutes

½ cup each canned whole
    green, wax, kidney,
    Italian green, and
    garbanzo beans

1 cup wine vinegar

½ cup sugar

1 medium onion

2 tablespoons olive oil

Easily extended for a main dish by adding canned tuna or salmon, or cooked shrimp.

1. Drain the beans and place them in a large salad bowl.

2. In a small saucepan, combine the wine vinegar and sugar; heat over low heat until the sugar is completely dissolved. Add to the beans.

3. Thinly slice the onion, then cut the slices in half to make slivers. Add to the beans. Add the olive oil.

4. Toss the salad to mix all the ingredients well. Serve chilled.

NUTRITIONAL FACTS PER SERVING

Calories: 184	Protein: 4.5 g	Carbohydrates: 31 g
Calcium: 33 mg	Total Fat: 5 g (24% fat cals)	Saturated Fat: 0 g

EXCHANGES, PER SERVING: 2 Fruit; 1 Very Lean Meat; 1 Fat.

Mock Chopped Liver With String Beans

A wonderful dish, hard to discern from the "real thing."

Yield: 4 servings
Prep. time: 15 minutes

1. In a large saucepan, place the green beans and onion in about $\frac{1}{2}$ cup water. Bring the water to a boil over medium heat, then reduce the heat to low and simmer until the vegetables are soft, about 10 minutes. Remove the pan from the heat and add the eggs, walnuts, black pepper, and garlic. Mash until the mixture has the consistency of a pâté.

2. Serve cold with crackers.

4 cups green beans, cut into 1-inch lengths

1 small onion, chopped

2 hard-cooked eggs, chopped

1 tablespoon ground walnuts

Black pepper to taste

Chopped garlic to taste

NUTRITIONAL FACTS PER SERVING

Calories: 120   Protein: 7 g   Carbohydrates: 12 g
Calcium: 80 mg   Total Fat: 5 g (38% fat cals) Saturated Fat: 1 g

EXCHANGES, PER SERVING: 2 Vegetable; $\frac{1}{2}$ Very Lean Meat; 1 Fat.

Mock Chopped Liver With Lentils

Spread some on rye bread for an outstanding sandwich.

Yield: 4 servings
Prep. time: 10 minutes

1. In a large skillet, heat 1 teaspoon of the oil over medium heat. Add the onion and sauté until browned. Transfer the onion to a blender and add the lentils, egg, garlic powder, black pepper, remaining oil, and mayonnaise. Blend until the mixture has the consistency of a pâté.

2. Serve cold with crackers.

1 tablespoon oil

1 medium onion, finely chopped

1 cup cooked lentils, mashed

1 hard-cooked egg, mashed

Garlic powder to taste

Black pepper to taste

1 tablespoon reduced-fat mayonnaise

NUTRITIONAL FACTS PER SERVING

Calories: 125   Protein: 4.5 g   Carbohydrates: 12 g
Calcium: 17 mg   Total Fat: 5.5 g (39% fat cals) Saturated Fat: 0.5 g

EXCHANGES, PER SERVING: $\frac{1}{2}$ Very Lean Meat; $\frac{1}{2}$ Starch; 1 Fat.

Bean Enchiladas

Yield: 6 servings
Prep. time: 30 minutes
Broiling time: 1 minute

1 tablespoon oil

1 small onion, finely
   chopped

¾ teaspoon chopped garlic

1½ cups tomato sauce

12-ounce can pinto beans,
   drained

4-ounce can corn, drained

1 teaspoon chili powder

6 corn tortillas

¼ cup shredded nondairy
   Cheddar cheese

A perennial South-of-the-Border favorite that also is a meal-in-one.

1. In a large skillet, heat the oil over medium heat. Add the onion and garlic, and sauté until soft, about 2 minutes. Add the tomato sauce, pinto beans, corn, and chili powder; stir well. Bring the mixture to a boil, then reduce the heat and simmer for 20 minutes.

2. Preheat the broiler. Lightly coat a 12-x-9-inch baking pan with nonstick cooking spray.

3. Spoon ⅙ of the bean filling into the center of 1 of the tortillas. Sprinkle with 2 teaspoons of the grated cheese. Roll the tortilla up around the filling and place seam-side down in the baking pan. Repeat with the remaining tortillas and filling.

4. Place the pan under the broiler for 1 minute to heat the enchiladas. Serve immediately.

NUTRITIONAL FACTS PER SERVING

Calories: 300	Protein: 15 g	Carbohydrates: 48 g
Calcium: 260 mg	Total Fat: 7.5 g (22% fat cals)	Saturated Fat: 2 g

---

EXCHANGES, PER SERVING: 1 Very Lean Meat; 3 Starch; 1½ Fat.

Beans With Tortillas

A vegetarian entrée that includes calcium and protein.

Yield: 4 servings
Prep. time: 35 minutes

1. Preheat the oven to 350°F.

2. In a medium bowl, combine the kidney beans, vinegar, and chili powder; let stand for 10 minutes.

3. In a large skillet, melt the margarine over medium heat. Add the green pepper and onions, and sauté until the onions start to brown. Add the bean mixture and heat for another 5 minutes.

4. Meanwhile, wrap the tortillas in foil. Place the wrapped tortillas in the oven for 5 minutes to heat and soften.

5. Remove the tortillas from the oven. Spoon $\frac{1}{8}$ of the bean filling into the center of 1 of the tortillas. Top with 2 tablespoons of the sour cream and 2 tablespoons of the cucumber. Roll the tortilla up around the filling and place seam-side down on a serving plate. Repeat with the remaining tortillas and filling. Serve immediately.

1 cup canned kidney beans, drained

1 tablespoon vinegar

1 teaspoon chili powder

1 tablespoon nondairy margarine

$\frac{1}{2}$ cup chopped green pepper

$\frac{1}{2}$ cup chopped onion

8 corn tortillas

1 cup nondairy sour cream

1 cup chopped cucumber

NUTRITIONAL FACTS PER SERVING (2 TORTILLAS)

Calories: 230	Protein: 8.5 g	Carbohydrates: 33 g
Calcium: 161 mg	Total Fat: 7 g (27% fat cals)	Saturated Fat: 1.1 g

EXCHANGES, PER SERVING (2 TORTILLAS): $\frac{1}{2}$ Very Lean Meat; 1 Starch; 1 Fruit; $\frac{1}{2}$ Vegetable; 1 Fat.

Vegetable Burgers

Yield: 6 servings
Prep. time: 10 minutes
Baking time: 15 minutes

2 cups canned kidney
  beans, drained, 1/4 cup
  liquid reserved

1/4 cup grated carrot

1 medium onion, chopped

Black pepper to taste

1/2 cup oat bran

1/4 cup tomato sauce

2 tablespoons olive oil

A vegetarian burger.

1. Preheat the oven to 350°F. Lightly coat a baking sheet with nonstick cooking spray.

2. In a blender, combine the kidney beans and 1/4 cup liquid, the carrots, the onion, and the black pepper. Blend until the mixture is smooth. Transfer the mixture to a large bowl. Add the oat bran, tomato sauce, and olive oil, and mix well.

3. Divide the mixture into 6 portions. Form the portions into patties. Arrange the patties on the baking sheet and place the sheet in the oven. Bake until the patties are browned, about 15 minutes.

4. Serve on hamburger buns with pickle relish.

NUTRITIONAL FACTS PER SERVING

Calories: 190	Protein: 8 g	Carbohydrates: 27 g
Calcium: 49 mg	Total Fat: 6 g (28% fat cals)	Saturated Fat: 0.6 g

EXCHANGES, PER SERVING: 1/2 Very Lean Meat; 1 Starch; 1/2 Fruit;
1 Vegetable; 1 Fat.

Pasta With Garbanzo Beans

Yield: 8 servings
Prep. time: 10 minutes

1 tablespoon nondairy
  margarine

1 medium onion, diced

1 medium green pepper,
  seeded and diced

2 cups canned garbanzo
  beans, drained

1-pound package macaroni,
  cooked according to
  package directions and
  drained

A complete meal when served with a vegetable salad.

1. In a large skillet, melt the margarine over medium heat. Add the onion and green pepper, and sauté until soft, about 3 minutes. Add the garbanzo beans and heat for 1 minute more. Add the cooked macaroni and toss.

2. Serve immediately.

NUTRITIONAL FACTS PER SERVING

Calories: 200	Protein: 7 g	Carbohydrates: 36 g
Calcium: 31 mg	Total Fat: 2.6 g (12% fat cals)	Saturated Fat: 0.3 g

EXCHANGES, PER SERVING: 1/2 Very Lean Meat; 1 Starch; 1 1/2 Fruit;
1/2 Fat.

Tofu Kebabs

One example of the versatility of the Asian staple tofu.

1. If using wooden skewers, soak them in water in a shallow pan for 1 hour to prevent them from burning on the grill.

2. Squeeze the water out of the tofu and cut the tofu into 1-inch cubes. Place the cubes in a small bowl.

3. In a separate bowl, combine the honey and soy sauce; mix well. Pour the marinade over the tofu cubes, then toss the tofu to coat it.

4. Thread the tofu onto the skewers, alternating the tofu cubes with the green pepper quarters, onions, and cherry tomatoes.

5. Heat the grill to medium-low and lightly oil the grate. Cook the tofu and vegetables, turning frequently and basting with the marinade, until they are golden brown and tender, about 10 minutes.

6. Serve with boiled rice.

Yield: 4 servings
Prep. time: 20 minutes

1 pound firm tofu

2 tablespoons honey

2 tablespoons soy sauce

1 green pepper, cut into quarters and seeded

4 small onions, peeled

4 cherry tomatoes, trimmed

NUTRITIONAL FACTS PER SERVING

Calories: 170	Protein: 15 g	Carbohydrates: 15 g
Calcium: 148 mg	Total Fat: 6 g (32% fat cals)	Saturated Fat: 1 g

EXCHANGES, PER SERVING: 1 Medium Fat Meat; 3 Vegetable.

Pasta Primavera

Yield: 4 servings
Prep. time: 10 minutes

1 tablespoon olive oil

1 cup cooked broccoli florets

1 tablespoon dried basil

½ teaspoon minced garlic

½ teaspoon dried oregano

Black pepper to taste

8-ounce package spaghetti,
cooked according to
package directions and
drained

A low-fat version of a popular Italian entrée.

1. In a large skillet, heat the olive oil over medium heat. Add the broccoli florets and sauté for 3 to 4 minutes. Add the basil, garlic, oregano, and black pepper; toss to mix. Add the pasta and toss.

2. Serve hot.

NUTRITIONAL FACTS PER SERVING

Calories: 250	Protein: 8 g	Carbohydrates: 43 g
Calcium: 58 mg	Total Fat: 4.4 g (16% fat cals)	Saturated Fat: 0.6 g

EXCHANGES, PER SERVING: 3 Starch; 1 Fat.

Macaroni and Fruit Salad

Yield: 6 servings
Prep. time: 5 minutes

2 cups cubed unpeeled
apple

1 teaspoon lemon juice

1 cup seedless green grapes

1 cup chopped celery

8-ounce package macaroni,
cooked according to
package directions and
drained

¼ cup reduced-fat
mayonnaise

¼ cup nondairy sour cream

¼ cup coarsely chopped
walnuts

A colorful summertime favorite with an interesting mixture of textures and flavors.

1. In a large bowl, toss the apple cubes with the lemon juice. Add the grapes, celery, macaroni, mayonnaise, and sour cream, and gently mix. Place in the refrigerator for at least 1 hour.

2. Add the walnuts and serve chilled.

NUTRITIONAL FACTS PER SERVING

Calories: 290	Protein: 8 g	Carbohydrates: 47 g
Calcium: 38 mg	Total Fat: 8.6 g (27% fat cals)	Saturated Fat: 1.3 g

EXCHANGES, PER SERVING: 2 Starch; 1 Fruit; 1½ Fat.

Spaghetti With Honey and Sesame Seeds

Sweet, creamy, and an unusual way to serve spaghetti.

Yield: 6 servings
Prep. time: 5 minutes

1. In a large saucepan, combine the soymilk, honey, and sesame or poppy seeds. Heat over low heat for 2 to 3 minutes. Add the spaghetti and toss.

2. Serve hot.

½ cup nonfat soymilk

¼ cup honey

¼ cup sesame or poppy seeds

4 cups cooked thin spaghetti, drained

NUTRITIONAL FACTS PER SERVING

Calories: 270	Protein: 9 g	Carbohydrates: 49 g
Calcium: 28 mg	Total Fat: 3.5 g (12% fat cals)	Saturated Fat: 0 g

EXCHANGES, PER SERVING: 3 Starch; ½ Fat.

Spaghetti and Tuna Casserole

A perfect meal when served with a green vegetable.

Yield: 8 servings
Prep. time: 15 minutes
Baking time: 30 minutes

1. Preheat the oven to 350°F. Lightly coat a 1½-quart casserole dish with nonstick cooking spray.

2. In a large saucepan, melt the margarine over low heat. Add the flour, garlic, and black pepper; stir to blend. Add the milk, stirring constantly until the mixture has thickened. Add the tuna and spaghetti, and toss.

3. Turn the mixture into the casserole dish. Sprinkle with the bread crumbs. Place the dish in the oven and bake until the mixture has browned, about 30 minutes.

4. Serve hot with cooked Brussels sprouts.

2 tablespoons nondairy margarine

2 tablespoons all-purpose flour

½ teaspoon minced garlic

Black pepper to taste

1 cup reduced-lactose skim milk

13-ounce can water-packed tuna, drained

8-ounce package spaghetti, cooked according to package directions and drained

1 cup dairy-free bread crumbs

NUTRITIONAL FACTS PER SERVING

Calories: 210	Protein: 17 g	Carbohydrates: 23 g
Calcium: 55 mg	Total Fat: 4.5 g (19% fat cals)	Saturated Fat: 0 g

EXCHANGES, PER SERVING: 2 Very Lean Meat; 1½ Starch; 1 Fat.

Vegetable Manicotti

Yield: 8 servings
Prep. time: 55 minutes
Baking time: 35 minutes

16 manicotti shells, cooked
   according to package
   directions and drained

FILLING

1 tablespoon oil

10-ounce package frozen
   chopped spinach,
   thawed and drained

2 cups mashed soft tofu

1 egg, beaten

2 tablespoons egg substitute

SAUCE

1 tablespoon oil

½ cup chopped onion

½ teaspoon minced garlic

4 cups canned tomatoes,
   drained and chopped

1 teaspoon dried oregano

Lower in calories and fat than the cheese-filled original, and well worth the extra minutes to prepare.

1. *To prepare the filling:* In a small skillet, heat the oil over medium heat. Add the spinach and sauté until limp. In a large bowl, combine the tofu, egg, and egg substitute; mix. Add the spinach and mix again. Set aside.

2. *To prepare the sauce:* In a large saucepan, heat the oil over medium heat. Add the onions and garlic, and sauté about 3 minutes. Add the tomatoes and oregano, and stir. Bring to a boil, then reduce the heat and simmer, uncovered, for 30 minutes. Set aside.

3. Preheat the oven to 350°F. Lightly coat a 13-x-9-inch baking pan with nonstick cooking spray.

4. Stuff the manicotti shells with the spinach-tofu filling, dividing the filling evenly among the shells.

5. Pour ½ of the sauce into the bottom of the baking pan. Use a rubber spatula or spoon to spread the sauce to the edges and into the corners. Arrange the stuffed manicotti in the pan. Top with the remaining sauce and cover the pan with foil. Place in the oven and bake until the sauce is bubbly, about 35 minutes. Serve immediately.

NUTRITIONAL FACTS PER SERVING (2 MANICOTTI)

Calories: 340	Protein: 16 g	Carbohydrates: 50 g
Calcium: 163 mg	Total Fat: 8 g (21% fat cals)	Saturated Fat: 0.8 g

---

EXCHANGES, PER SERVING (2 MANICOTTI): 1 Lean Meat;
1 Medium Fat Meat; 3 Starch; 1 Vegetable.

Noodles With Almonds

An Eastern European delicacy with a delightful mixture of textures.

1. In a large skillet, melt the margarine over medium heat. Add the almonds and sauté for 1 minute. Add the cooked noodles and toss.

2. Serve hot with meat or fish.

Yield: 6 servings
Prep. time: 5 minutes

1 tablespoon nondairy margarine

3 tablespoons slivered almonds

12-ounce package broad noodles, cooked according to package directions and drained

---

NUTRITIONAL FACTS PER SERVING

Calories: 268	Protein: 8 g	Carbohydrates: 45 g
Calcium: 34 mg	Total Fat: 6.5 g (22% fat cals)	Saturated Fat: 1.2 g

EXCHANGES, PER SERVING: 3 Starch; 1 Fat.

Noodle Pudding

One of my family's favorites. It also works well as a main dish.

1. Preheat the oven to 350°F. Lightly coat a 1½-quart casserole dish with nonstick cooking spray.

2. In a large bowl, cream the sugar and margarine with the back of a spoon. Add the cottage cheese, raisins, lemon juice, and lemon rind; mix. In a separate bowl, combine the egg yolks and egg substitute; beat until thick. Add to the cottage cheese mixture. Add the noodles and toss to mix. In a clean separate bowl, beat the egg whites with an electric mixer at medium speed until stiff but not dry; fold into the cottage cheese mixture.

3. Turn the mixture into the casserole dish. Place the casserole dish in a baking pan and fill the pan with hot water halfway up the side of the casserole dish. Place the pan with the casserole dish in the oven and bake until the pudding is golden brown, about 1 hour.

4. Serve as an entrée or a side dish.

Yield: 8 servings
Prep. time: 20 minutes
Baking time: 1 hour

½ cup sugar

1 tablespoon nondairy margarine, softened

1 cup reduced-lactose cottage cheese

¼ cup raisins

1 tablespoon lemon juice

Grated rind of ½ lemon

2 eggs, separated

½ cup egg substitute

8-ounce package broad noodles, cooked according to package directions and drained

---

NUTRITIONAL FACTS PER SERVING

Calories: 228	Protein: 11 g	Carbohydrates: 37 g
Calcium: 38 mg	Total Fat: 4 g (16% fat cals)	Saturated Fat: 1 g

EXCHANGES, PER SERVING: ½ Very Lean Meat; 2½ Starch; 1 Fat.

8

Poultry

An excellent source of protein and the B vitamins, poultry is a valuable
part of a healthful diet. Chicken is the most popular food bird,
with virtually every cuisine in the world using this ingredient
in some of its most popular dishes. Many of these recipes–including the
perennial favorites Chicken Cordon Bleu and Chicken Paprikash–
are presented in this chapter.

While the majority of recipes in the following pages feature chicken,
delicious variations are possible using turkey.
Other kinds of poultry–such as duck, goose, or Cornish game hen–
can also be used. No matter what kind of bird you choose,
however, remember that the meat must be cooked through, with no pink showing.
In addition, all utensils, dishes, and work surfaces that come in contact
with the raw meat should be washed immediately after use.

Oven-Fried Chicken

Yield: 6 servings
Prep. time: 15 minutes
Baking time: 1 hour

3 pounds chicken pieces, skinned

½ cup reduced-fat Italian salad dressing

Black pepper to taste

1 cup finely crushed bran flakes

A family favorite that lets you "fry" chicken the easy (and healthy) way—by baking it!

1. Preheat the oven to 450°F. Lightly coat a shallow baking pan with nonstick cooking spray.

2. Dip each chicken piece in the salad dressing and drain. Sprinkle with the black pepper and roll in the crushed bran flakes.

3. Arrange the chicken in the baking pan, leaving space between the pieces. Cover the pan tightly with foil. Place in the oven and bake until the chicken is tender, about 30 minutes. Remove the foil and bake until the chicken is browned, about 15 minutes more.

4. Serve with mashed sweet potatoes.

NUTRITIONAL FACTS PER SERVING

Calories: 253	Protein: 30 g	Carbohydrates: 19 g
Calcium: 34 mg	Total Fat: 5 g (18% fat cals)	Saturated Fat: 1.2 g

EXCHANGES, PER SERVING: 4 Very Lean Meat; 1 Starch; 1 Fat.

Chicken in Yogurt Sauce

Yield: 6 servings
Prep. time: 40 minutes

3 pounds chicken pieces, skinned

2 tablespoons all-purpose flour

2 tablespoons oil

½ cup nonpasteurized fat-free plain yogurt

¼ cup chicken bouillon

The yogurt enhances the mild flavor of the chicken.

1. Dust the chicken pieces with the flour.

2. In a large skillet, heat the oil over low heat. Add the chicken and sauté until tender, about 20 minutes. Drain the fat from the pan and let the chicken cool in the skillet for 10 minutes.

3. Add the yogurt and bouillon to the skillet. Bring the sauce to a boil over medium heat, then lower the heat and simmer for about 3 minutes.

4. Serve over brown rice.

NUTRITIONAL FACTS PER SERVING

Calories: 199	Protein: 31 g	Carbohydrates: 4 g
Calcium: 42 mg	Total Fat: 7 g (30% fat cals)	Saturated Fat: 1 g

EXCHANGES, PER SERVING: 4 Very Lean Meat.

Chicken in Cognac

The cognac gives an aromatic flavor to this creamed chicken dish.

Yield: 6 servings
Prep. time: 35 minutes

1. Spray a large skillet with nonstick cooking spray. Add the chicken and slowly brown both sides of the chicken breasts over low heat. Remove from the skillet.

2. Melt the margarine in the skillet. Add the mushrooms and garlic, and sauté until lightly browned.

3. Return the chicken to the skillet. Add the cognac and simmer until the chicken is tender, about 10 minutes. Remove the chicken from the skillet using a slotted spoon and arrange it on a serving platter. Cover to keep warm.

4. In a small bowl, combine the bouillon and cornstarch. Add to the pan juices and mix well. Bring the mixture to a boil over medium heat, then reduce the heat and simmer until thick, about 1 to 2 minutes. Stir in the cream and heat until the sauce thickens slightly, about 1 minute more. Add the lemon juice, stir, and pour over the chicken. Serve immediately.

6 white meat chicken cutlets (about 3 ounces each)

2 teaspoons nondairy margarine

1 cup sliced mushrooms

½ teaspoon garlic

½ cup cognac

½ cup chicken bouillon

1 teaspoon cornstarch

¼ cup nondairy cream

2 teaspoons lemon juice

NUTRITIONAL FACTS PER SERVING

Calories: 185	Protein: 27 g	Carbohydrates: 2 g
Calcium: 15 mg	Total Fat: 3 g (15% fat cals)	Saturated Fat: 1.1 g

EXCHANGES, PER SERVING: 4 Very Lean Meat.

Chicken Cordon Bleu

Yield: 6 servings
Prep. time: 45 minutes

6 white meat chicken cutlets (about 2 ounces each)

6 thin slices turkey ham (about 2 x 3 inches each)

6 thin slices nondairy mozzarella cheese (about ⅓ ounce each)

2 teaspoons oil

¼ teaspoon dried thyme

⅔ cup chicken bouillon

¼ cup cognac

¼ cup lemon juice

Black pepper to taste

The flavors of the chicken and the cheese blend together in this classic French presentation.

1. Pound the chicken breasts to a ¼-inch thickness. On top of each breast, arrange 1 slice of ham and 1 slice of cheese. Roll up the chicken breasts, tuck in the ends, and secure with toothpicks.

2. In a large skillet, heat the oil over low heat. Add the rolled-up chicken breasts and brown on all sides.

3. When browned, sprinkle the chicken with the thyme. Pour the bouillon over the chicken, raise the heat, and bring to a boil. Reduce the heat, cover the skillet, and simmer until the chicken is tender, about 15 minutes.

4. Remove the chicken from the skillet using a slotted spoon, and arrange it on a serving platter. Cover to keep warm.

5. Add the cognac, lemon juice, and black pepper to the pan liquid. Raise the heat to medium, bring to a boil, and cook until the liquid is reduced to half its original volume. Pour over the chicken.

6. Serve with polenta.

NUTRITIONAL FACTS PER SERVING

Calories: 220	Protein: 28 g	Carbohydrates: 6 g
Calcium: 145 mg	Total Fat: 4 g (16% fat cals)	Saturated Fat: 2.9 g

---

EXCHANGES, PER SERVING: 4 Very Lean Meat; 1 Vegetable; 1 Fat.

Chicken Fricassee

The brown sauce enhances the subtle taste of the chicken.

1. Preheat the oven to 350°F. Lightly coat a shallow baking pan with nonstick cooking spray.

2. On a plate or in a bowl, combine the flour, paprika, and black pepper. Add the chicken pieces 1 at a time, turning to coat well.

3. In a large skillet, heat the oil over medium heat. Add the chicken and brown on both sides. Transfer to the baking pan.

4. In a small bowl, combine the Brown Sauce and the water; mix well. Pour over the chicken. Place the chicken in the oven and bake until tender, about 50 minutes.

5. Serve with asparagus spears.

Yield: 6 servings
Prep. time: 25 minutes
Baking time: 50 minutes

¾ cup all-purpose flour

½ teaspoon paprika

Black pepper to taste

1½ pounds bite-sized skinless boneless chicken pieces

1 tablespoon oil

½ cup Brown Sauce (see page 66)

2 tablespoons water

NUTRITIONAL FACTS PER SERVING

Calories: 210	Protein: 21 g	Carbohydrates: 11 g
Calcium: 19 mg	Total Fat: 4 g (17% fat cals)	Saturated Fat: 1 g

EXCHANGES, PER SERVING: 3 Very Lean Meat; ½ Starch; 1 Fat.

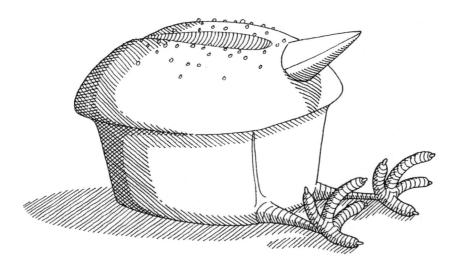

Chicken Paprikash

Yield: 6 servings
Prep. time: 1 hour 30 min.

3 pounds white meat
  chicken pieces, skinned

2 tablespoons paprika

2 tablespoons oil

1 onion, thinly sliced

1 cup chicken bouillon

¼ cup water

1 tablespoon cornstarch

Paprika is the unique spice that gives this dish its name.

1. Heavily dust the chicken pieces with the paprika.

2. In a large skillet, heat the oil over medium heat. Add the onion and sauté until transparent. Add the chicken and brown lightly, turning frequently. Add the bouillon, cover, reduce the heat, and simmer until the chicken is tender, about 1 hour.

3. In a small bowl, combine the water and cornstarch. Stir to make a smooth paste. Stir several tablespoons of the pan liquid into the cornstarch mixture, then add the cornstarch mixture to the skillet. Continue to simmer, stirring constantly, until the gravy has thickened.

4. To serve, line a platter with cooked penne. Remove the chicken from the skillet using a slotted spoon and arrange it over the penne. Pour the gravy over the chicken and serve immediately.

NUTRITIONAL FACTS PER SERVING

Calories: 197	Protein: 27 g	Carbohydrates: 2 g
Calcium: 20 mg	Total Fat: 5 g (22% fat cals)	Saturated Fat: 0 g

---

EXCHANGES, PER SERVING: 4 Very Lean Meat; 1 Fat.

Chicken Paprikash With Vegetables

An attractive one-dish meal, based on a universal favorite.

Yield: 6 servings
Prep. time: 1 hour 15 min.

1. In a large skillet, heat the oil over medium heat. Add the chicken pieces and sauté until browned on both sides. Remove them from the skillet and keep warm.

2. Add the bouillon, potatoes, onion, and carrot to the skillet. Reduce the heat and cook for 10 minutes, stirring occasionally.

3. Add the paprika. Remove the skillet from the heat and stir in the tomato sauce and flour. Return the skillet to the heat, raise the heat to medium, and bring the tomato sauce to a boil. Reduce the heat and simmer for 15 minutes.

4. Add the chicken pieces and simmer for 30 minutes more.

5. Just before serving, add the soymilk and stir. Garnish with the parsley and serve with noodles.

2 tablespoons oil

3 pounds split chicken breasts, skinned

1 cup chicken bouillon

2 small potatoes, cut into 1-inch cubes

1 onion, chopped

1 carrot, sliced

2 tablespoons paprika

1 cup tomato sauce

3 tablespoons all-purpose flour

1 cup reduced-fat soymilk

½ teaspoon chopped parsley, as garnish

NUTRITIONAL FACTS PER SERVING

Calories: 253	Protein: 30 g	Carbohydrates: 8 g
Calcium: 52 mg	Total Fat: 6 g (21% fat cals)	Saturated Fat: 0 g

EXCHANGES, PER SERVING: 4 Very Lean Meat; ½ Starch; 1 Fat.

Chicken à la King

Yield: 6 servings
Prep. time: 20 minutes

3 tablespoons low-fat
   nondairy margarine

3 tablespoons all-purpose
   flour

1½ cups chicken bouillon

½ cup dry white wine

1 teaspoon chopped garlic

Black pepper to taste

2 cups diced cooked white
   meat chicken

2 tablespoons oil

1 cup sliced mushrooms

½ cup chopped green
   pepper

½ cup chopped red pepper

Turkey can be substituted with excellent results.

1. In a large saucepan, melt the margarine over low heat. Add the flour, stirring constantly. Add the bouillon, wine, garlic, and black pepper. Stir constantly until smooth and thickened. Add the chicken.

2. In a large skillet, heat the oil over medium heat. Add the mushrooms, green pepper, and red pepper. Sauté until the peppers are soft, about 3 minutes.

3. Add the sautéed vegetables to the chicken mixture and heat, stirring gently, until hot, about 1 to 2 minutes.

4. Serve over rice.

NUTRITIONAL FACTS PER SERVING

Calories: 120	Protein: 14 g	Carbohydrates: 5 g
Calcium: 16.5 mg	Total Fat: 7 g (17% fat cals)	Saturated Fat: 0 g

EXCHANGES, PER SERVING: 2 Very Lean Meat; 1 Vegetable; 1 Fat.

Chicken Sandwich Spread

Yield: 6 servings
Prep. time: 10 minutes

2 cups diced cooked chicken

½ cup chopped green
   pepper

¼ cup reduced-fat
   mayonnaise

¼ cup chopped red pepper

2 tablespoons
   reduced-lactose skim milk

1 teaspoon onion powder

Black pepper to taste

Also a hit served with crackers on the buffet table.

1. In a blender, combine all the ingredients. Purée until smooth.

2. Serve with whole wheat or rye bread for sandwiches.

NUTRITIONAL FACTS PER SERVING

Calories: 119	Protein: 14 g	Carbohydrates: 2.2 g
Calcium: 13.6 mg	Total Fat: 5.2 g (39% fat cals)	Saturated Fat: 1.6 g

EXCHANGES, PER SERVING: 1 Very Lean Meat; 1 Lean Meat; ½ Fat.

Chicken and Rice Casserole

Pineapple chunks or cranberry sauce make a great garnish for this one-dish meal.

1. Preheat the oven to 375°F. Lightly coat a large skillet and a baking pan with nonstick cooking spray.

2. In the skillet, heat the margarine over medium heat. Add the chicken pieces and sauté until browned on both sides.

3. Transfer the chicken to the baking pan. Add the rice, soymilk, bouillon, and black pepper. Cover, place in the oven, and bake until the chicken is tender, about 20 minutes.

4. Serve with cooked julienne carrots or coleslaw.

Yield: 8 servings
Prep. time: 20 minutes
Baking time: 20 minutes

3 tablespoons nondairy margarine

4 pounds split chicken breasts, skinned and boned

1 cup uncooked white rice

1 cup reduced-fat soymilk

1 cup chicken bouillon

Black pepper to taste

NUTRITIONAL FACTS PER SERVING

Calories: 235 Protein: 29 g Carbohydrates: 6 g
Calcium: 29 mg Total Fat: 6 g (23% fat cals) Saturated Fat: 1 g

EXCHANGES, PER SERVING: 4 Very Lean Meat; 1 Vegetable; 1 Fat.

Curried Chicken Salad

The combination of curry and Mock Sour Cream With a Twist gives this salad an unusual tangy taste.

1. In a blender, combine all the ingredients. Purée until smooth. Transfer to a small bowl and place in the refrigerator for at least 1 hour.

2. Serve chilled.

Yield: 3 servings
Prep. time: 10 minutes

1 cup diced cooked chicken

¼ cup chopped celery

2 tablespoons chopped green onion

2 tablespoons Mock Sour Cream With a Twist (see page 63)

2 tablespoons reduced-fat mayonnaise

1 teaspoon curry powder

NUTRITIONAL FACTS PER SERVING

Calories: 160 Protein: 15 g Carbohydrates: 3.6 g
Calcium: 23 mg Total Fat: 3.5 g (20% fat cals) Saturated Fat: 0 g

EXCHANGES, PER SERVING: 1 Very Lean Meat; 1 Lean Meat;
½ Vegetable; 1 Fat.

Chicken Tetrazzini

Yield: 8 servings
Prep. time: 1 hour

2 tablespoons nondairy
    margarine

¼ cup all-purpose flour

1¾ cups chicken bouillon

¾ cup reduced-fat soymilk

2 tablespoons egg substitute

3 cups shredded cooked
    chicken

1 cup sliced mushrooms

¼ cup dry sherry

8-ounce package spaghetti,
    cooked according to
    package directions and
    drained

Accompany this dish with a mandarin orange salad for color.

1. Preheat the broiler. Lightly coat a large skillet and a baking pan with nonstick cooking spray.

2. In the skillet, melt the margarine over medium heat. Remove the skillet from the heat and add the flour; stir until smooth. Add the bouillon, return the skillet to the heat, and bring the mixture to a boil. Reduce the heat and simmer until the sauce has thickened. Remove from the heat and allow to cool for about 15 minutes.

3. Once the sauce has cooled, add the soymilk and egg substitute. Place the skillet over low heat and stir. Add the chicken, mushrooms, and sherry. Heat gently, stirring constantly, for 10 minutes.

4. Arrange the spaghetti to cover the entire bottom of the baking pan. Top with the chicken-sauce mixture. Place under the broiler and brown quickly, for about 1 minute. Serve immediately.

NUTRITIONAL FACTS PER SERVING

Calories: 220	Protein: 22 g	Carbohydrates: 10 g
Calcium: 24 mg	Total Fat: 8 g (32% fat cals)	Saturated Fat: 2 g

---

EXCHANGES, PER SERVING: 1½ Very Lean Meat; 1½ Lean Meat;
½ Starch; 1 Fat.

Chinese Chicken

A tasty recipe adapted from the Chinese.

Yield: 5 servings
Prep. time: 30 minutes

1. In a small bowl, combine the bouillon, soy sauce, sherry, and cornstarch. Stir until smooth.

2. In a large skillet, heat the oil over medium heat. Add the chicken and sauté until browned. Remove the chicken from the skillet and keep warm.

3. Add the mushrooms, celery, and garlic to the skillet. Sauté, stirring constantly, until the mushrooms are slightly browned, about 2 minutes.

4. Return the chicken to the skillet. Add the water chestnuts and bamboo shoots. Stir the sauce again and pour over the skillet mixture. Cook until the chicken and the vegetables are tender, about 2 to 3 minutes.

5. Serve with rice or angel hair pasta.

½ cup chicken bouillon

¼ cup soy sauce

2 tablespoons dry sherry

1 tablespoon cornstarch

1 tablespoon oil

2 cups cubed white meat chicken (1-inch cubes)

1 cup sliced mushrooms

½ cup sliced celery

1 teaspoon minced garlic

1 cup water chestnuts

½ cup bamboo shoots

NUTRITIONAL FACTS PER SERVING

Calories: 160   Protein: 22 g   Carbohydrates: 4 g
Calcium: 10 mg   Total Fat: 3 g (17% fat cals)   Saturated Fat: 0 g

EXCHANGES, PER SERVING: 3 Very Lean Meat; 1 Vegetable; ½ Fat.

Chicken Tortillas

Yield: 4 servings
Prep. time: 20 minutes

8 cornmeal or flour tortillas

2 teaspoons oil

½ cup chopped onion

½ cup chopped green
  pepper

1 cup diced cooked chicken

2 teaspoons Worcestershire
  sauce

1 teaspoon chili powder

1 cup nonpasteurized
  fat-free plain yogurt

1 cup chopped tomato

A tantalizing entrée adapted from popular South-of-the-Border cuisine.

1. Preheat the oven to 350°F.

2. Wrap the tortillas in foil and place in the oven for 5 minutes. Remove from the oven and keep warm.

3. In a large skillet, heat the oil over medium heat. Add the onions and green peppers, and sauté until the onions are soft.

4. Add the chicken, Worcestershire sauce, and chili powder to the skillet. Sauté for 2 to 3 minutes more.

5. Spoon ⅛ of the chicken filling into the center of 1 of the tortillas. Roll up the tortilla around the filling and place seam-side down on a serving platter. Repeat with the remaining tortillas and filling.

6. Top each rolled-up tortilla with 2 tablespoons of the yogurt and 2 tablespoons of the tomato. Serve immediately.

NUTRITIONAL FACTS PER SERVING (2 TORTILLAS)

Calories: 318	Protein: 24 g	Carbohydrates: 40 g
Calcium: 218 mg	Total Fat: 7.5 g (23% fat cals)	Saturated Fat: 0 g

---

EXCHANGES, PER SERVING (2 TORTILLAS): 1 Very Lean Meat;
1 Lean Meat; 2 Starch; 2 Vegetables; 1 Fat.

Turkey Croquettes

An excellent way to use leftover Thanksgiving turkey—and great for chicken leftovers, as well.

Yield: 8 servings
Prep. time: 1 hour

1. In a medium saucepan, melt the margarine over low heat. Add the flour and stir. Add the milk and stir. Stir constantly until slightly thickened, about 2 to 3 minutes; do not boil. Remove from the heat and allow to cool to room temperature.

2. When the mixture has cooled, add the turkey, the $\frac{1}{4}$ cup egg substitute, and the black pepper. Mix well.

3. Divide the mixture into 8 parts. Form each part into a patty with a 4-inch diameter. Brush the patties with the remaining egg substitute and roll in the bread crumbs.

4. In a large skillet, heat the oil over medium heat. Add the patties and sauté until golden brown on both sides.

5. Serve with cooked kale.

2 tablespoons low-fat nondairy margarine

$\frac{1}{4}$ cup all-purpose flour

1 cup reduced-lactose skim milk

3 cups finely chopped cooked turkey

$\frac{1}{4}$ cup egg substitute

Black pepper to taste

2 tablespoons egg substitute

1 cup dairy-free bread crumbs

2 tablespoons oil

NUTRITIONAL FACTS PER SERVING

Calories: 250	Protein: 23 g	Carbohydrates: 18 g
Calcium: 80 mg	Total Fat: 6 g (21% fat cals)	Saturated Fat: 0 g

EXCHANGES, PER SERVING: $1\frac{1}{2}$ Very Lean Meat; $1\frac{1}{2}$ Lean Meat; 1 Starch.

Stuffed Cornish Hens

Yield: 4 servings
Prep. time: 30 minutes
Roasting time: 1 hour 30 min.

2 tablespoons low-fat
    nondairy margarine

1 small onion, chopped

1 cup soft dairy-free bread
    cubes

2 large celery ribs, chopped

1 tablespoon chopped
    parsley

$\frac{1}{2}$ teaspoon poultry
    seasoning

Black pepper to taste

2 Cornish hens (about
    1–1$\frac{1}{2}$ pounds each)

Garlic powder to taste

Poultry seasoning to taste

Paprika to taste

2 cups water

1 teaspoon chicken bouillon
    powder, undiluted

1 tablespoon all-purpose
    flour

$\frac{1}{2}$ cup nonpasteurized
    fat-free plain yogurt

Formal dining at its best.

1. Preheat the oven to 350°F. Lightly coat a medium skillet and a shallow roasting pan with nonstick cooking spray.

2. In the skillet, melt the margarine over medium heat. Add the onion and sauté until transparent. Add the bread, celery, parsley, $\frac{1}{2}$ teaspoon poultry seasoning, and black pepper. Mix well.

3. Season the cavities of the Cornish hens with the garlic powder. Stuff each hen with about $\frac{1}{2}$ cup of the bread mixture. Secure the openings with skewers, fasten the neck skin to the back with skewers, and tie the legs together with string. Rub the hens with the poultry seasoning and paprika to taste.

4. Place the hens breast sides up in the roasting pan. Fashion aluminum foil into tents over them. Place in the oven and roast until the drumsticks move easily when touched, about 45 to 60 minutes.

5. Remove the foil and roast until the hens are browned, about 15 to 30 minutes more.

6. Remove the hens from the oven. Remove the skin. Cut each in half along the backbone. Place the 4 halves on a serving platter. Cover to keep warm.

7. In a small saucepan, combine the water and bouillon powder. Add the flour and stir until smooth. Stir in the yogurt. Pour over the hens. Serve immediately.

NUTRITIONAL FACTS PER SERVING

Calories: 310	Protein: 27 g	Carbohydrates: 32 g
Calcium: 116 mg	Total Fat: 7 g (20% fat cals)	Saturated Fat: 1 g

---

EXCHANGES, PER SERVING: 1$\frac{1}{2}$ Very Lean Meat; 1$\frac{1}{2}$ Lean Meat;
2 Starch.

9

Fish

Fish and shellfish are excellent sources of protein and the B vitamins. The relatively low fat content of most fish, along with the desirable and beneficial polyunsaturated oils in fish, explains why this food is so important. And now, the judicious use of nondairy cream and soymilk will permit you to enjoy these foods in dishes such as Creamed Fish and Salmon Newburg.

Please note that the recipes in this section using canned fish employ water-packed varieties. If you choose to use an oil-packed product, first rinse the fish with water.

Baked Fish

Yield: 4 servings
Prep. time: 10 minutes
Baking time: 20 minutes

1 pound perch fillets

1 tablespoon melted
    nondairy margarine

$\frac{1}{2}$ cup chopped onion

1 tablespoon lemon juice

$\frac{1}{4}$ teaspoon paprika

2 tablespoons dairy-free
    bread crumbs, as garnish

1 tablespoon chopped
    parsley, as garnish

A quick way to prepare a favorite fish with a crunch.

1. Preheat the oven to 350°F. Lightly coat a shallow baking pan and a small skillet with nonstick cooking spray.

2. In the baking pan, arrange the fillets in a single layer, skin side down.

3. In the skillet, heat $\frac{1}{2}$ tablespoon of the melted margarine over medium heat. Add the onions and sauté until transparent. Transfer to a small bowl and add the remaining margarine, the lemon juice, and the paprika; mix. Spoon the mixture over the fillets.

4. Place the fish in the oven and bake, uncovered, until it flakes easily with a fork, about 20 minutes.

5. Remove the fish from the oven and garnish with the bread crumbs and parsley. Serve immediately.

NUTRITIONAL FACTS PER SERVING

Calories: 170	Protein: 26 g	Carbohydrates: 3 g
Calcium: 154 mg	Total Fat: 5.5 g (29% fat cals)	Saturated Fat: 0.7 g

---

EXCHANGES, PER SERVING: 4 Very Lean Meat.

Curried Fish

Curry adds an exotic zing to this dish.

Yield: 4 servings
Prep. time: 40 minutes

1. In a large skillet, melt the margarine over medium heat. Add the onions and garlic, and sauté for 3 to 5 minutes.

2. Add the curry powder to the skillet and mix well. Add the tomatoes and sauté gently until tender.

3. When the tomatoes are tender, remove the pan from the heat and crush the tomatoes using a spoon. Return the pan to the heat, add the lemon juice, and simmer for 4 to 5 minutes.

4. Add the fish to the skillet, arranging it in a single layer and covering it with the sauce. Bring to a boil, cover, and simmer for 10 minutes.

5. Serve sprinkled with the parsley.

1 tablespoon nondairy margarine

1 medium onion, chopped

½ teaspoon minced garlic

1 teaspoon curry powder

2 medium tomatoes, sliced

1 tablespoon lemon juice

1 pound turbot or flounder fillets, cut into serving-size pieces

1 tablespoon chopped parsley, as garnish

NUTRITIONAL FACTS PER SERVING

Calories: 170   Protein: 26.5 g   Carbohydrates: 4.8 g
Calcium: 31 mg   Total Fat: 4.7 g (25% fat cals)   Saturated Fat: 0.9 g

EXCHANGES, PER SERVING: 3½ Very Lean Meat; 1 Vegetable.

Creamed Fish

Yield: 4 servings
Prep. time: 40 minutes

1 tablespoon nondairy
   margarine

1 cup sliced fresh
   mushrooms

1 medium onion, finely
   chopped

1 pound flounder, pollack,
   or haddock fillets

$\frac{1}{2}$ cup dry white wine

1 tablespoon lemon juice

1 tablespoon all-purpose
   flour

2 tablespoons nondairy
   cream

$\frac{1}{4}$ teaspoon white pepper

Serve this modified version of a classic French dish with sweet potatoes and asparagus for picture-book appeal.

1. In a large skillet, melt $\frac{1}{2}$ tablespoon of the margarine over medium heat. Add the mushrooms and onions, and sauté until the mushrooms are tender, about 3 minutes. Transfer to a small bowl.

2. Arrange the fish in the skillet in a single layer. Add the wine, lemon juice, and just enough water to cover the fish. Bring to a boil, then reduce the heat, cover, and simmer until the fish flakes easily with fork, about 4 to 5 minutes. Remove the fish from the skillet using a slotted spoon and arrange it on a serving platter. Cover to keep warm.

3. Bring the liquid remaining in the skillet back to a boil, and continue to cook until it is reduced to 1 cup, about 15 minutes. Pour it into a measuring cup.

4. Place the remaining margarine in the skillet and melt over low heat. Add the flour and stir for 1 minute. Remove the skillet from the heat and stir in the reserved liquid and the cream. Return the skillet to the heat and bring the mixture to a boil, stirring constantly. Stir in the mushroom mixture and the white pepper. Pour the sauce over the fish and serve immediately.

NUTRITIONAL FACTS PER SERVING

Calories: 186	Protein: 27 g	Carbohydrates: 5.6 g
Calcium: 30 mg	Total Fat: 5.5 g (27% fat cals)	Saturated Fat: 0.9 g

EXCHANGES, PER SERVING: $3\frac{1}{2}$ Very Lean Meat; 1 Vegetable.

Fish With Yogurt

Easy to prepare and scrumptious—a terrific combination of tastes.

1. Preheat the oven to 350°F. Lightly coat a shallow baking pan and a small skillet with nonstick cooking spray.

2. Cut the fish fillets into 4 equal servings. Pat them dry with paper toweling. Arrange them in the baking pan in a single layer.

3. In the skillet, melt the margarine over medium heat. Add the mushrooms and onion, and sauté for about 3 minutes. Spoon over the fish.

4. Sprinkle the fish with the black pepper. Spread with the yogurt, then sprinkle with the bread crumbs. Place in the oven and bake, uncovered, until the fish flakes easily with a fork, about 25 to 30 minutes.

5. Remove the fish from the oven and garnish with the paprika. Serve immediately.

Yield: 4 servings
Prep. time: 15 minutes
Baking time: 25–30 min.

1 pound pollack fillets

1 tablespoon nondairy margarine

1 cup sliced fresh mushrooms

1 small onion, chopped

Black pepper to taste

½ cup nonpasteurized fat-free plain yogurt

2 tablespoons dairy-free bread crumbs

Paprika, as garnish

NUTRITIONAL FACTS PER SERVING

Calories: 175	Protein: 31 g	Carbohydrates: 5.6 g
Calcium: 87 mg	Total Fat: 4 g (21% fat cals)	Saturated Fat: 0.7 g

EXCHANGES, PER SERVING: 4 Very Lean Meat; 1 Vegetable.

Fish Florentine

Yield: 6 servings
Prep. time: 10 minutes
Baking time: 20–25 min.

1 tablespoon nondairy
   margarine

2 tablespoons all-purpose
   flour

Ground nutmeg to taste

White pepper to taste

1 cup reduced-fat soymilk

10-ounce package frozen
   chopped spinach,
   thawed and drained

1 tablespoon lemon juice

1 pound haddock, halibut,
   or flounder fillets

2 tablespoons grated
   nondairy Parmesan
   cheese, as garnish

1/8 teaspoon paprika, as
   garnish

Tastes as good as it looks. This dish is outstanding served with potato pancakes.

1. Preheat the oven to 350°F. Lightly coat a small skillet and a shallow baking pan with nonstick cooking spray.

2. In the skillet, melt the margarine over low heat. Add the flour, nutmeg, and white pepper, and stir to blend. Simmer, stirring constantly, until smooth and bubbly. Remove the skillet from the heat and stir in the soymilk. Return the skillet to the heat, raise the heat to medium, and bring the mixture to a boil. Reduce the heat and simmer, stirring constantly, until thickened, about 3 minutes. Remove the skillet from the heat.

3. Place the spinach in the baking pan, spreading it out to cover the bottom of the pan. Sprinkle with the lemon juice. Arrange the fish on the spinach in a single layer, then spread the sauce over the fish and spinach. Place in the oven and bake until the fish flakes easily with a fork, about 20 to 25 minutes.

4. Remove the fish from the oven and sprinkle it with the cheese and paprika. Serve immediately.

NUTRITIONAL FACTS PER SERVING

Calories: 170	Protein: 25 g	Carbohydrates: 5.5 g
Calcium: 235 mg	Total Fat: 5 g (27% fat cals)	Saturated Fat: 1.6 g

---

EXCHANGES, PER SERVING: 3 Very Lean Meat; 1 Vegetable.

Fish Veronique

A truly splendid dish fit for a king—or any other special guest.

1. Season the fish with the black pepper and place it in a large skillet. Add the water, wine, onions, and lemon juice, and bring to a boil over medium heat. Cover, reduce the heat, and simmer until the fish flakes easily with a fork, about 4 to 5 minutes. Remove the fish from the skillet using a slotted spoon and arrange it on a serving platter. Cover to keep warm.

2. Add the grapes to the liquid remaining in the skillet. Raise the heat to medium and bring the pan liquid back to a boil. Reduce the heat and simmer, uncovered, for about 3 minutes. Remove the grapes and set aside. Continue to simmer the pan liquid until it is reduced to 1 cup. Add the Sherried White Sauce and stir.

3. To serve, spoon the sauce over the fish and garnish with the reserved grapes. Serve immediately.

Yield: 6 servings
Prep. time: 45 minutes

1½ pounds flounder or haddock fillets

Black pepper to taste

1 cup water

¼ cup dry white wine

2 tablespoons finely chopped onion

1 tablespoon lemon juice

1 cup seedless green or white grapes

6 tablespoons Sherried White Sauce (see page 70)

NUTRITIONAL FACTS PER SERVING

Calories: 168	Protein: 27.5 g	Carbohydrates: 5 g
Calcium: 25 mg	Total Fat: 2 g (11% fat cals)	Saturated Fat: 0.3 g

EXCHANGES, PER SERVING: 4 Very Lean Meat.

VERONICA LAKE

Sautéed Fish in Pungent Sauce

Yield: 8 servings
Prep. time: 35 minutes

1½ pounds fish fillets
(haddock works well)

2 tablespoons oil

¾ cup water

2 carrots, thinly sliced

2 small onions, sliced

1 small green pepper,
seeded and cut into rings

1 tablespoon packed brown
sugar

¾ teaspoon ground ginger

1 clove garlic, minced

⅛ cup white vinegar

2 tablespoons cornstarch

As good as any served in the best Chinese restaurants.

1. Cut the fish fillets into 8 equal servings. Pat them dry with paper toweling.

2. In a large skillet, heat the oil over medium heat. Add the fish fillets in a single layer and cook until they flake easily with a fork, about 10 minutes. Remove the fish from the skillet and arrange it on a serving platter. Cover to keep warm.

3. In a medium saucepan, combine the water, carrots, onions, green pepper, brown sugar, ginger, and garlic. Bring to a boil over medium heat, then reduce the heat, cover, and simmer for 5 minutes.

4. In a measuring cup, combine the vinegar and cornstarch. Mix well and stir into the vegetables. Bring the vegetable mixture back to a boil and simmer, stirring constantly, for 1 minute. Pour over the fish.

5. Serve with rice.

NUTRITIONAL FACTS PER SERVING

Calories: 155	Protein: 20.7 g	Carbohydrates: 3.6 g
Calcium: 40 mg	Total Fat: 5.8 g (34% fat cals)	Saturated Fat: 0.8 g

EXCHANGES, PER SERVING: 3 Very Lean Meat; ½ Vegetable.

Stuffed Sole

Delicious, attractive, and mild tasting.

Yield: 6 servings
Prep. time: 25 minutes
Baking time: 15 min.

1. Preheat the oven to 425°F. Lightly coat a small skillet and a shallow baking pan with nonstick cooking spray.

2. In the skillet, heat the oil over medium heat. Add the mushrooms and sauté until limp. Add the spinach and sauté for 1 minute more. Remove the skillet from the heat and drain out the oil. Add the garlic powder and oregano and toss the vegetables to mix.

3. Place $\frac{1}{6}$ of the vegetable mixture in the center of each fillet. Roll up the fillets and place seam-side down in the baking pan. Sprinkle with the lemon juice.

4. Place the fish in the oven and bake for 15 minutes. Sprinkle with the cheese and bake for 1 minute more. Garnish with the paprika and serve immediately.

2 teaspoons oil

½ pound mushrooms, sliced

½ pound spinach, chopped

¼ teaspoon garlic powder

¼ teaspoon dried oregano

6 sole fillets (about 3 ounces each)

4 teaspoons lemon juice

2 tablespoons grated nondairy mozzarella cheese

Paprika, as garnish

NUTRITIONAL FACTS PER SERVING

Calories: 150	Protein: 28 g	Carbohydrates: 1.5 g
Calcium: 63 mg	Total Fat: 3 g (18% fat cals)	Saturated Fat: 1 g

EXCHANGES, PER SERVING: 4 Very Lean Meat.

Salmon Newburg

Yield: 5 servings
Prep. time: 45 minutes

1 tablespoon low-fat
   nondairy margarine

1 tablespoon grated onion

3 tablespoons all-purpose
   flour

1 teaspoon paprika

Black pepper to taste

1½ cups reduced-fat soymilk

⅛ teaspoon Tabasco sauce

14¾-ounce can
   water-packed salmon,
   drained

1 tablespoon chopped fresh
   parsley

½ cup egg substitute

3 tablespoons cognac

2 tablespoons nondairy
   cream

My family's favorite seafood dish for the past forty years.

1. In a large saucepan, melt the margarine over medium heat. Add the onion and sauté for 5 minutes. Blend in the flour, paprika, and black pepper. Gradually stir in the soymilk and Tabasco sauce. Bring to a boil, then reduce the heat and simmer, stirring constantly, until thick and smooth, about 10 minutes.

2. Flake the salmon and add to the saucepan along with the parsley. Simmer for 3 minutes more.

3. In a small bowl, combine the egg substitute with the cognac and cream. Mix well. Add to the salmon mixture and simmer for an additional 2 minutes.

4. Serve with rice or noodles.

NUTRITIONAL FACTS PER SERVING

Calories: 353	Protein: 27 g	Carbohydrates: 5 g
Calcium: 344 mg	Total Fat: 15 g (38% fat cals)	Saturated Fat: 1.3 g

---

EXCHANGES PER SERVING: 4 Lean Meat; ½ Fat.

Getting the Fat Out of Your Meals

While eliminating lactose-containing products from your dishes will allow you to enjoy your meals without discomfort, a truly healthy dish is not just free of problem ingredients, but is high in nutrients and low in the fat that can compromise your health. In fact, accepted dietary guidelines suggest limiting fat consumption so that no more than 30 percent of your daily intake of calories comes from fat. Here are some tips for reducing fat when you cook.

• When making pancakes, waffles, and egg dishes, replace whole eggs with egg whites or fat-free egg substitutes.

• When preparing beef or poultry dishes, buy the leanest cuts available, remove the skin before cooking, and trim off any visible fat.

Salmon Divan

Many chicken recipes can be modified to use salmon. This recipe is a successful adaptation of Chicken Divan.

1. Preheat the oven to 450°F. Lightly coat a shallow baking pan and a small skillet with nonstick cooking spray.

2. In the baking pan, arrange the broccoli in 1 layer. Flake the salmon and mash the bones. Spread the salmon over the broccoli.

3. In the skillet, melt the margarine over medium heat. Blend in the flour and black pepper. Gradually stir in the milk. Bring to a boil, then reduce the heat and simmer, stirring constantly, until thickened. Stir in the sherry. Pour the sauce over the broccoli and salmon. Place in the oven and bake for 15 to 20 minutes. Serve hot.

Yield: 5 servings
Prep. time: 25 minutes
Baking time: 15–20 min.

20-ounce package frozen broccoli spears, cooked according to package directions and drained

14¾-ounce can water-packed salmon, drained

1 tablespoon low-fat nondairy margarine

2 tablespoons all-purpose flour

Black pepper to taste

1 cup lactose-free skim milk

2 tablespoons sherry

NUTRITIONAL FACTS PER SERVING

Calories: 190	Protein: 20 g	Carbohydrates: 6 g
Calcium: 226 mg	Total Fat: 10 g (47% fat cals)	Saturated Fat: 1.3 g

EXCHANGES, PER SERVING: 2½ Lean Meat; 1 Vegetable; ½ Fat.

• When browning or sautéing meats and vegetables, use nonstick pans, and spray them with nonstick cooking spray instead of using the usual oil or margarine. If your food still sticks to the pan, add a small amount of water, broth, or wine.

• When browning ground beef for chili or a casserole dish, drain off any fat before adding the beef to your recipe.

• When making soup, skim off the fat when it rises to the top. Better yet, chill the soup in the refrigerator, and remove the hardened fat before reheating.

• When making gravy with meat drippings, defat the drippings by placing them in a fat-separator cup. If you don't have one of these devices, pour the drippings into a bowl, add a few ice cubes, and skim off the fat once it rises and hardens.

Salmon Loaf

Yield: 5 servings
Prep. time: 15 minutes
Baking time: 30 min.

14³⁄₄-ounce can
  water-packed salmon,
  drained

½ cup dairy-free bread
  crumbs

¼ cup chopped green onion

¼ cup egg substitute

2 tablespoons chopped
  fresh parsley

½ teaspoon celery salt

Black pepper to taste

1 cup tomato sauce

The leftovers are great for a lunch box or a quickie meal.

1. Preheat the oven to 350°F. Lightly coat a 9-x-5-inch loaf pan with nonstick cooking spray.

2. In a large bowl, flake the salmon and mash the bones. Add the bread crumbs, green onion, egg substitute, parsley, celery salt, and black pepper; mix well. Turn the mixture into the loaf pan. Place the pan in the oven and bake until the loaf is set, about 30 minutes.

3. In a small saucepan, heat the tomato sauce.

4. Remove the loaf from the oven and immediately turn it out onto a serving platter. Allow to set for a few minutes before slicing. Serve with the tomato sauce.

NUTRITIONAL FACTS PER SERVING

Calories: 220	Protein: 21 g	Carbohydrates: 6 g
Calcium: 235 mg	Total Fat: 9 g (37% fat cals)	Saturated Fat: 1.3 g

---

EXCHANGES, PER SERVING: 3 Lean Meat; 1 Vegetable.

Tuna Alaska

For that extra-special breakfast or lunch.

Yield: 2 servings
Prep. time: 20 minutes

1. Preheat the broiler.

2. In a small bowl, combine the tuna, yogurt, lemon juice, mayonnaise, green onion, dillweed, and black pepper. Mix well. Spread ½ of the mixture on each slice of toast.

3. In a separate bowl, beat the egg white until stiff but not dry. Spread over the tuna salad.

4. Place the open-face sandwiches under the broiler. Broil until the meringue is lightly browned. Serve immediately.

7-ounce can water-packed tuna, drained

2 tablespoons nonpasteurized plain yogurt

2 tablespoons lemon juice

1 tablespoon reduced-fat mayonnaise

1 tablespoon minced green onion

¼ teaspoon dried dillweed

Black pepper to taste

2 slices dairy-free bread, toasted

1 egg white

NUTRITIONAL FACTS PER SERVING

Calories: 220	Protein: 28 g	Carbohydrates: 15 g
Calcium: 133 mg	Total Fat: 4.5 g (18% fat cals)	Saturated Fat: 1.4 g

EXCHANGES, PER SERVING: 3½ Very Lean Meat; 1 Starch; 1 Fat.

Fish Salad

A different fish salad. The lemon and dill flavors complement the flavor of the fish.

Yield: 4 servings
Prep. time: 5 minutes

1. In a medium bowl, flake the cod. Add the celery, lemon juice, dillweed, and black pepper; mix. Add the mayonnaise and mix thoroughly.

2. Serve cold on a bed of lettuce.

1 pound cod, cooked

½ cup chopped celery

2 tablespoons lemon juice

¼ teaspoon dried dillweed

Black pepper to taste

3 tablespoons reduced-fat mayonnaise

NUTRITIONAL FACTS PER SERVING

Calories: 163	Protein: 21 g	Carbohydrates: 1 g
Calcium: 20 mg	Total Fat: 2 g (11% fat cals)	Saturated Fat: 0 g

EXCHANGES, PER SERVING: 3 Very Lean Meat.

Shrimp Puffs

Yield: 4 servings
Prep. time: 10 minutes

6 ounces chopped cooked shrimp

½ cup reduced-fat mayonnaise

½ teaspoon lemon juice

2 egg whites

4 slices dairy-free bread, toasted

4 lemon wedges

Perfect for a buffet table.

1. Preheat the broiler.

2. In a medium bowl, combine the shrimp, mayonnaise, and lemon juice.

3. In a separate bowl, beat the egg whites until stiff but not dry. Fold into the shrimp mixture.

4. Spread ¼ of the mixture on each slice of toast. Place under the broiler until browned, about 20 to 30 seconds.

5. Serve hot with the lemon wedges.

NUTRITIONAL FACTS PER SERVING

Calories: 160	Protein: 11 g	Carbohydrates: 15 g
Calcium: 65 mg	Total Fat: 6.9 g (39% fat cals)	Saturated Fat: 0 g

---

EXCHANGES, PER SERVING: 1 Very Lean Meat; 1 Starch; 1 Fat.

Salmon-Cucumber Salad

Yield: 5 servings
Prep. time: 15 minutes

2 cucumbers

Black pepper to taste

14¾-ounce can water-packed salmon, drained

½ cup nonpasteurized fat-free plain yogurt

1 tablespoon lemon juice

2 tablespoons minced green onion, as garnish

A perfect summer treat—pretty and nutritious.

1. Quarter the cucumbers lengthwise, seed them, and cut the quarters into thin slices. Place them in a medium bowl and sprinkle with the pepper. Drain them well.

2. Flake the salmon and mash the bones. Add the salmon to the cucumbers. Mix lightly.

3. In a small bowl, mix the yogurt with the lemon juice. Pour over the salmon mixture.

4. Garnish with the onion, and serve.

NUTRITIONAL FACTS PER SERVING

Calories: 180	Protein: 22 g	Carbohydrates: 3.8 g
Calcium: 200 mg	Total Fat: 9 g (45% fat cals)	Saturated Fat: 0 g

---

EXCHANGES, PER SERVING: 3 Lean Meat; ½ Vegetable.

Dilled Shrimp Salad

Tastes best when prepared several hours before serving.

1. In a blender, combine all the ingredients. Blend until smooth. Transfer to a serving bowl and place in the refrigerator for at least 1 hour.

2. Serve well chilled with crackers or pita bread.

Variation

Substitute a white fish, such as cod or sole, for the shrimp.

Yield: 3 servings
Prep. time: 5 minutes

2 cups chopped cooked shrimp

½ cup chopped celery

2 tablespoons chopped green onion

2 tablespoons finely chopped green pepper

2 tablespoons nondairy cream

2 tablespoons reduced-fat mayonnaise

1 tablespoon lemon juice

1 teaspoon dried dillweed

Black pepper to taste

NUTRITIONAL FACTS PER SERVING

Calories: 170 Protein: 22 g Carbohydrates: 3 g
Calcium: 77 mg Total Fat: 5.2 g (28% fat cals) Saturated Fat: 0.9 g

EXCHANGES, PER SERVING: 3 Very Lean Meat; 1 Fat.

Shrimp With Pea Pods

The pea pods give a unique, crunchy texture to this colorful dish.

1. In a medium bowl, combine the shrimp, pea pods, tofu, and green onion. Add the soy sauce and sesame oil, and mix gently. Place in the refrigerator for at least 1 hour.

2. Serve well chilled with cold cooked rice.

Yield: 4 servings
Prep. time: 10 minutes

8 ounces fresh or frozen raw shrimp, peeled, deveined, and boiled

6-ounce package frozen Chinese pea pods, cooked according to package directions and drained

4 ounces firm tofu, drained and cut into ½-inch slices

½ cup finely chopped green onion

2 tablespoons soy sauce

1 tablespoon sesame oil

NUTRITIONAL FACTS PER SERVING

Calories: 140 Protein: 16.5 g Carbohydrates: 6 g
Calcium: 102 mg Total Fat: 5.6 g (36% fat cals) Saturated Fat: 1.2 g

EXCHANGES, PER SERVING: 2 Very Lean Meat; 1 Vegetable; 1 Fat.

Scallops Supreme

Yield: 4 servings
Prep. time: 45 minutes
Baking time: 15 min.

1 teaspoon oil

1 cup sliced mushrooms

¼ cup minced onion

2 tablespoons finely
    chopped green onion

1 clove garlic, minced

1 pound scallops, cut into
    ½-inch pieces

½ cup all-purpose flour

½ cup dry white wine

¼ cup water

⅛ teaspoon dried dillweed

¼ cup nondairy cream

2 teaspoons lemon juice

Black pepper to taste

An appealing, flavorful dish with the subtle taste of scallops.

1. Preheat the oven to 350°F.

2. In a large saucepan, heat the oil over medium heat. Add the mushrooms, onion, green onion, and garlic. Sauté for 5 minutes.

3. Dip the scallops in the flour and add to the pan. Sauté until lightly browned.

4. Add the wine, water, and dillweed. Bring to a boil, then reduce the heat and simmer for 5 minutes.

5. Remove the vegetables and scallops from the pan using a slotted spoon. Divide them evenly among 4 individual ovenproof serving dishes. Keep warm.

6. Simmer the sauce remaining in the pan until it is thick.

7. When the sauce has thickened, add the cream, lemon juice, and black pepper. Stir and pour over the 4 servings of vegetables and scallops. Place the 4 dishes in the oven for 15 minutes. Serve hot.

NUTRITIONAL FACTS PER SERVING

Calories: 169	Protein: 18 g	Carbohydrates: 9 g
Calcium: 26 mg	Total Fat: 4 g (21% fat cals)	Saturated Fat: 0.3 g

---

EXCHANGES, PER SERVING: 2 Very Lean Meat; ½ Starch; 1 Fat.

10

Beef and Lamb

Beef is the mainstay of many a hearty meal–just think of an inviting bowl of goulash served on a winter's evening! But while beef is an excellent source of protein, it also contains somewhat more saturated fat than does poultry. To cut down on fat, use lean or less marbled cuts. Also, trim off any visible fat before cooking and use nonstick cooking spray when sautéing. Browning beef before cooking–a common step in many recipes– caramelizes the meat's proteins and sugars on its surface, increasing the flavor. Browning also liquefies the fat, enabling you to drain it off.

Lamb is flavorful and tender and also the star of many hearty dishes. Two lamb recipes, one Greek, round out this chapter of meat offerings.

Braised Beef

Yield: 8 servings
Prep. time: 2 hours

1½ pounds round steak

3 tablespoons all-purpose flour

1 tablespoon low-fat nondairy margarine

2 cups beef bouillon

3 carrots, sliced

2 medium onions, sliced

¼ teaspoon dried thyme

Black pepper to taste

¼ cup Mock Sour Cream With a Twist (see page 63)

A most satisfying dish that can be easily stretched by adding more carrots and onions.

1. Sprinkle 1 side of the round steak with half of the flour and pound the flour in. Flip the round steak, sprinkle the other side with the remaining flour, and pound the flour in. Cut the steak into 1-inch cubes.

2. In a large skillet, melt the margarine over medium heat. Add the beef and sauté until browned on all sides, about 15 minutes. Drain the fat out of the skillet.

3. Add the bouillon and bring to a boil. Reduce the heat, cover the skillet, and simmer the mixture for 15 minutes.

4. Add the carrots and onions. Sprinkle on the thyme and black pepper. Cover the skillet and simmer until the beef and vegetables are tender, about 40 to 60 minutes.

5. Remove the skillet from the heat and stir in the Mock Sour Cream With a Twist.

6. Serve with wild rice.

NUTRITIONAL FACTS PER SERVING

Calories: 215	Protein: 26.5 g	Carbohydrates: 6 g
Calcium: 28 mg	Total Fat: 8 g (33% fat cals)	Saturated Fat: 2.8 g

EXCHANGES, PER SERVING: 3½ Lean Meat; 1 Vegetable.

Goulash

A favorite cold-weather dish.

Yield: 8 servings
Prep. time: 45 minutes

1. In a large skillet, melt the margarine over medium heat. Add the beef and sauté until browned on all sides, about 15 minutes. Remove the beef using a slotted spoon and place it on several layers of paper toweling to drain.

2. Add the onions and garlic to the skillet. Sauté until the onions are tender.

3. Drain the fat from the skillet. Add the water, paprika, bouillon powder, and black pepper. Return the beef to the skillet. Bring the mixture to a boil, then reduce the heat, cover the skillet, and simmer until the beef is tender, about $1\frac{1}{2}$ hours.

4. In a small bowl, combine the water with the cornstarch. Stir until smooth, then stir into the beef mixture. Raise the heat to medium and bring the mixture to a boil, stirring constantly. Boil and stir for 1 minute, then reduce the heat.

5. Stir in the yogurt and heat the mixture to serving temperature.

6. Serve with fettuccine.

1 tablespoon low-fat nondairy margarine

$1\frac{1}{2}$ pounds round steak, cut into 1-inch cubes

2 medium onions, chopped

1 clove garlic, chopped

3 cups water

2 tablespoons paprika

2 teaspoons chicken bouillon powder, undiluted

Black pepper to taste

$\frac{1}{4}$ cup cold water

2 tablespoons cornstarch

$\frac{1}{2}$ cup nonpasteurized fat-free plain yogurt

NUTRITIONAL FACTS PER SERVING

Calories: 200	Protein: 25 g	Carbohydrates: 4 g
Calcium: 24 mg	Total Fat: 7.7 g (34% fat cals)	Saturated Fat: 2.7 g

EXCHANGES, PER SERVING: 3 Lean Meat; $\frac{1}{2}$ Vegetable.

Skewered Beef and Tofu

Yield: 6 servings
Prep. time: 1 hour 20 min.

¾ pound round steak, cut
   into 1-inch cubes

½ pound firm tofu, drained
   and cut into 1½-inch
   cubes

¼ cup soy sauce

6 small onions

6 cherry tomatoes

6 pieces green pepper
   (1½-inch squares)

6 canned unsweetened
   pineapple chunks

A summertime entrée that can also be prepared on the grill.

1. If using wooden skewers, soak them in water in a shallow pan for 1 hour to prevent them from burning under the broiler.

2. In a small bowl, marinate the beef and tofu in the soy sauce for 1 hour.

3. Remove the beef and tofu from the soy sauce using a slotted spoon. Set the soy sauce aside.

4. Preheat the broiler. Thread the beef and tofu onto the skewers, alternating them with the onions, tomatoes, green pepper, and pineapple.

5. Grill the kebabs under the broiler, basting frequently with the soy sauce. Cook until the beef is tender, about 10 minutes.

6. Remove the kebabs from the broiler and place on a large serving platter. Serve immediately.

NUTRITIONAL FACTS PER SERVING

Calories: 170	Protein: 19 g	Carbohydrates: 9.8 g
Calcium: 59 mg	Total Fat: 6 g (32% fat cals)	Saturated Fat: 2 g

EXCHANGES, PER SERVING: 2 Lean Meat; 2 Vegetable.

Beef Burgundy

The rich color and flavor come from the wine.

1. In a large skillet, melt the margarine over medium heat. Add the onions and sauté until transparent.

2. Add the beef and sauté until browned on all sides, about 15 minutes.

3. Add the flour and black pepper. Stir until smooth. Add the bouillon and wine, and stir again. Bring the mixture to a boil, then reduce the heat and simmer for $2\frac{1}{2}$ hours.

4. Add the mushrooms and simmer for 30 minutes more. Add additional bouillon if necessary.

5. Stir in the yogurt.

6. Serve with a tossed green salad.

1 tablespoon low-fat nondairy margarine

1 small onion, sliced

$1\frac{1}{2}$ pounds round steak, cut into 1-inch cubes

2 tablespoons all-purpose flour

Black pepper to taste

1 cup beef bouillon

1 cup Burgundy wine

1 cup fresh mushrooms

1 cup nonpasteurized fat-free plain yogurt

NUTRITIONAL FACTS PER SERVING

Calories: 190	Protein: 21 g	Carbohydrates: 4.6 g
Calcium: 69 mg	Total Fat: 9 g (42% fat cals)	Saturated Fat: 2.5 g

EXCHANGES, PER SERVING: 3 Lean Meat; 1 Vegetable.

Szechuan Pepper Beef

Yield: 5 servings
Prep. time: 1 hour 5 min.

1½ tablespoons soy sauce

1½ tablespoons hoisin
  sauce

1 tablespoon
  Worcestershire sauce

2 slices ginger root

Black pepper to taste

1 pound lean flank steak,
  cut into 2-x-¼-inch slices

1 tablespoon low-fat
  nondairy margarine

1 green pepper, cut into
  1-inch squares

An example of an excellent Chinese dairy-free dish.

1. In a large bowl, combine the soy sauce, hoisin sauce, Worcestershire sauce, ginger root, and black pepper; stir. Add the beef, cover the bowl, and let the beef marinate for about 1 hour, turning it occasionally.

2. In a large skillet, heat the margarine over medium heat. Remove the beef from the marinade using a slotted spoon and place it in the skillet. Sauté for 2 minutes, then turn and sauté for 1 minute more.

3. Add the green pepper and the marinade, and cook for 30 seconds.

4. Serve over rice.

NUTRITIONAL FACTS PER SERVING

Calories: 185	Protein: 22 g	Carbohydrates: 1 g
Calcium: 8 mg	Total Fat: 10 g (49% fat cals)	Saturated Fat: 3.5 g

---

EXCHANGES, PER SERVING: 3 Lean Meat.

Wiener Schnitzel

Yield: 4 servings
Prep. time: 1 hour

½ cup nonfat soymilk

2 tablespoons egg substitute

2 tablespoons grated
  nondairy Parmesan
  cheese

2 tablespoons all-purpose
  flour

1-pound veal roast,
  trimmed, boned, and cut
  into 4 slices

2 tablespoons low-fat
  nondairy margarine

Black pepper to taste

A well-accepted version of a dish borrowed from Austria.

1. In a small bowl, combine the soymilk with the egg substitute and Parmesan cheese. Place the flour in a large bowl.

2. Pound the veal slices to a ¼-inch thickness. Dip each veal slice first in the flour, then in the soymilk mixture.

3. In a large skillet, melt the margarine over medium heat. Add the veal slices and sauté until browned on both sides. Cover the skillet, lower the heat, and cook until tender, about 20 minutes.

4. Season with the black pepper and serve garnished with lemon slices.

NUTRITIONAL FACTS PER SERVING

Calories: 230	Protein: 26 g	Carbohydrates: 1 g
Calcium: 71 mg	Total Fat: 10.5 g (41% fat cals)	Saturated Fat: 3.5 g

---

EXCHANGES, PER SERVING: 3½ Lean Meat.

Beef Stroganoff

Baked acorn squash is an attractive accompaniment to this hearty dish.

1. In a large skillet, melt 1 tablespoon of the margarine over low heat. Add the mushrooms, onions, and garlic, and stir. Cover the skillet and cook the vegetables, stirring occasionally, until the onions are tender, about 5 to 10 minutes. Remove the vegetables and any liquid from the skillet and set aside.

2. In the skillet, melt the remaining margarine over medium heat. Add the beef and sauté, stirring constantly, until browned on all sides, about 10 minutes.

3. Add the water, bouillon powder, and black pepper. Heat the mixture to boiling, then reduce the heat, cover the skillet, and simmer until the beef is tender, about 10 to 15 minutes.

4. Return the vegetable mixture to the skillet. Raise the heat and bring the mixture to a boil, then reduce the heat. Stir in the wine, then the Mock Sour Cream With a Twist. Heat just until hot.

5. Garnish with the parsley and serve with broad noodles.

Yield: 5 servings
Prep. time: 1 hour

2 tablespoons low-fat nondairy margarine

¼ cup sliced mushrooms

2 medium onions, sliced

1 clove garlic, finely chopped

1 pound beef tenderloin, sliced across the grain into ½-inch strips

½ cup water

1 teaspoon beef bouillon powder, undiluted

¼ teaspoon black pepper

1 cup Madeira wine

½ cup Mock Sour Cream With a Twist (see page 63)

½ teaspoon chopped parsley

NUTRITIONAL FACTS PER SERVING

Calories: 270   Protein: 24 g   Carbohydrates: 8 g
Calcium: 10.6 mg   Total Fat: 13.5 g (45% fat cals) Saturated Fat: 6 g

---

EXCHANGES, PER SERVING: 3 Lean Meat; ½ Starch; ½ Fat.

Ground Beef Stroganoff

Yield: 5 servings
Prep. time: 30 minutes

1 pound lean ground round beef

1 teaspoon oil

2 cups sliced mushrooms

½ cup chopped onion

1 teaspoon minced garlic

2 tablespoons all-purpose flour

1 cup chicken bouillon

½ cup dry red wine

1 cup nonpasteurized fat-free plain yogurt

The ground beef gives this traditional dish a new twist.

1. In a large skillet, brown the ground beef over medium-low heat. Remove the beef from the skillet using a slotted spoon, and drain the fat from the beef and the skillet. Set the beef aside and keep it warm.

2. In the skillet, heat the oil over medium heat. Add the mushrooms, onions, and garlic, and sauté until the mushrooms are browned, about 1 to 2 minutes.

3. Add the flour and stir until the mixture is well blended. Add the bouillon and wine, and stir again. Bring to a boil, then reduce the heat and simmer, stirring constantly, until the sauce is thickened and smooth.

4. Return the beef to the skillet and simmer for 5 minutes more.

5. Stir in the yogurt.

6. Serve over spinach noodles.

NUTRITIONAL FACTS PER SERVING

Calories: 250	Protein: 25 g	Carbohydrates: 7 g
Calcium: 93 mg	Total Fat: 12 g (43% fat cals)	Saturated Fat: 5 g

EXCHANGES, PER SERVING: 3 Lean Meat; ½ Starch; ½ Fat.

Meat Loaf

Sweet potatoes are an unusual addition that also adds vitamin A to the diet.

1. Preheat the oven to 350°F. Lightly coat a 9-x-5-inch loaf pan with nonstick cooking spray.

2. In a large bowl, combine the sweet potatoes, barbecue sauce, onions, and parsley; mix. Add the ground beef, corn flakes, egg substitute, and black pepper; mix thoroughly.

3. Turn the mixture into the loaf pan. Place the pan in the oven and bake until the loaf is set, about 1 hour.

4. Serve with green vegetables.

Yield: 5 servings
Prep. time: 10 minutes
Baking time: 1 hour

¼ cup mashed sweet potatoes

¼ cup barbecue sauce

2 tablespoons chopped onion

1 tablespoon chopped parsley

1 pound lean ground beef

½ cup crushed corn flakes

2 tablespoons egg substitute

Black pepper to taste

NUTRITIONAL FACTS PER SERVING

Calories: 305	Protein: 24 g	Carbohydrates: 17 g
Calcium: 11 mg	Total Fat: 14 g (41% fat cals)	Saturated Fat: 5.5 g

EXCHANGES, PER SERVING: 3 Medium Fat Meat; 1 Starch.

Quick and Easy Meat Loaf

The name almost says it all—it is also delicious!

1. Preheat the oven to 350°F. Lightly coat a 9-x-5-inch loaf pan with nonstick cooking spray.

2. In a large bowl, combine the ground turkey and egg substitute. Add the mashed potatoes, onion, garlic powder, and black pepper. Mix thoroughly.

3. Turn the mixture into the loaf pan. Place the pan in the oven and bake until the loaf is set, about 50 to 60 minutes.

4. Serve with tomato or mushroom sauce.

Yield: 5 servings
Prep. time: 5 minutes
Baking time: 1 hour

1 pound ground turkey

¼ cup egg substitute

½ cup mashed potatoes

2 tablespoons chopped onion

½ teaspoon garlic powder

Black pepper to taste

NUTRITIONAL FACTS PER SERVING

Calories: 175	Protein: 20 g	Carbohydrates: 4 g
Calcium: 20 mg	Total Fat: 5 g (26% fat cals)	Saturated Fat: 1.3 g

EXCHANGES, PER SERVING: 3 Very Lean Meat; 1 Fat.

Beef Casserole

Yield: 6 servings
Prep. time: 25 minutes
Baking time: 45 min.

1 pound lean ground round

1 onion, chopped

½ teaspoon minced garlic

1 cup tomato sauce

½ teaspoon dried basil

½ teaspoon dried oregano

6-ounce package noodles, cooked according to package directions and drained

¼ cup Mock Sour Cream With a Twist (see page 63)

Add a salad to make a complete meal.

1. Preheat the oven to 350°F. Lightly grease a rectangular 2-quart casserole dish.

2. In a large skillet, slowly brown the ground beef over low heat.

3. Add the onion and garlic, and cook for 2 minutes more.

4. Add the tomato sauce, basil, and oregano, and stir. Raise the heat to medium and bring the mixture to a boil, then reduce the heat and simmer until the sauce is thick.

5. In the casserole dish, arrange the noodles to cover the entire bottom. Top the noodles with the meat mixture. Place the casserole in the oven and bake until firm and browned, about 45 minutes.

6. Pour the Mock Sour Cream With a Twist over the casserole and serve immediately.

NUTRITIONAL FACTS PER SERVING

Calories: 260	Protein: 24.5 g	Carbohydrates: 26 g
Calcium: 41.5 mg	Total Fat: 8 g (28% fat cals)	Saturated Fat: 3 g

---

EXCHANGES, PER SERVING: 2 Lean Meat; 1½ Starch; ½ Vegetable.

Swedish Meatballs

An attractive addition to a buffet table.

Yield: 32 meatballs
Prep. time: 45 minutes

1. In a large bowl, combine the ground turkey, ground veal, mashed potatoes, egg substitute, onions, nutmeg, ginger, and black pepper. Mix well. Form into 1-inch balls.

2. Spray a large skillet with nonstick cooking spray. In the skillet, brown the meatballs over low heat, shaking the skillet occasionally to brown the meatballs all around.

3. Add the water, cover the skillet, and simmer the meatballs for 20 minutes.

4. Serve with mustard or barbecue sauce.

$3/4$ pound ground turkey

$1/2$ pound lean ground veal

1 cup mashed potatoes

$1/4$ cup egg substitute

2 tablespoons grated onion

$1/4$ teaspoon ground nutmeg

$1/8$ teaspoon ground ginger

Black pepper to taste

$1/4$ cup water

NUTRITIONAL FACTS PER SERVING (4 MEATBALLS)

Calories: 170	Protein: 19 g	Carbohydrates: 4.5 g
Calcium: 18 mg	Total Fat: 6 g (32% fat cals)	Saturated Fat: 2 g

---

EXCHANGES, PER SERVING (4 MEATBALLS): $1\frac{1}{2}$ Very Lean Meat;
1 Medium Fat Meat; 1 Vegetable; $\frac{1}{2}$ Fat.

Baked Veal Cutlets

Yield: 6 servings
Prep. time: 25 minutes
Baking time: 45 min.

1 cup crushed bran flakes

1 tablespoon chopped
parsley

1 teaspoon dried oregano

½ cup nonfat soymilk

2-pound veal roast,
trimmed, boned, and cut
into 6 slices

Baking instead of frying reduces the fat content and gives this dish a crispy character.

1. Preheat the oven to 350°F. Lightly coat a shallow baking pan with nonstick cooking spray.

2. In a small bowl, combine the bran flakes, parsley, and oregano. Pour the soymilk in a separate small bowl.

3. Pound the veal slices to a ¼-inch thickness. Dip each veal slice first in the soymilk, then in the bran flake mixture. Arrange the veal slices in a single layer in the baking pan. Place the pan in the oven and bake until the veal is tender, about 45 minutes.

4. Serve with broccoli.

NUTRITIONAL FACTS PER SERVING

Calories: 312	Protein: 24 g	Carbohydrates: 5 g
Calcium: 40 mg	Total Fat: 15 g (43% fat cals)	Saturated Fat: 4 g

---

EXCHANGES, PER SERVING: 3½ Medium Fat Meat.

Veal in Sour Cream

A tender and flavorful entrée, beautifully presented.

Yield: 8 servings
Prep. time: 40 minutes

1. In a large skillet, melt the margarine over medium heat. Dust 3 to 4 of the veal slices with the flour, and sauté until browned on both sides, about 2 to 4 minutes. Transfer to a plate and repeat with the remaining veal slices.

2. When all the veal has been browned and set aside, add the onions to the skillet. Sauté until transparent.

3. Add the mushrooms and sauté until tender, about 10 minutes more.

4. Remove the skillet from the heat, slowly add the cognac, then stir in the Mock Sour Cream With a Twist. Add the browned veal slices and heat for about 30 seconds.

5. Serve garnished with the apricot halves.

2 tablespoons low-fat nondairy margarine

12 slices veal roast (about 2 ounces each), trimmed and boned

3 tablespoons all-purpose flour

$\frac{1}{2}$ cup chopped onion

1 cup sliced mushrooms

$\frac{1}{4}$ cup cognac

$\frac{1}{2}$ cup Mock Sour Cream With a Twist (see page 63)

6 canned apricot halves, as garnish

NUTRITIONAL FACTS PER SERVING

Calories: 255	Protein: 25 g	Carbohydrates: 15 g
Calcium: 30 mg	Total Fat: 9.5 g (33% fat cals)	Saturated Fat: 3 g

EXCHANGES, PER SERVING: 3 Lean Meat; 1 Starch.

Creamy Lactose-Free Gravies

Being lactose-intolerant does not mean that you have to give up the creamy sour cream- or milk-based gravies you love so much. Instead of waving good-bye to your favorite Stroganoff dish, try the following:

• Stir Mock Sour Cream (page 62) or Mock Sour Cream With a Twist (page 63) into your dish, or into the pan juices, toward the end of the cooking time. Cook just until hot, and serve immediately.

• Stir nonpasteurized yogurt into your dish, or into the pan juices, at the end of the cooking time, and serve immediately. (Do not cook the yogurt, as this may cause it to curdle.)

• Stir soymilk into your dish, or into the pan juices, toward the end of the cooking time. Heat the mixture thoroughly, bringing it just to a boil. Serve immediately.

• Stir reduced-lactose milk into your dish, or into the pan juices, toward the end of the cooking time. Simmer the mixture until the volume is reduced and the gravy has thickened, and serve.

Cheeseless Veal Parmesan

Yield: 4 servings
Prep. time: 55 minutes
Baking time: 30 min.

8 slices veal roast (about
   1½ ounces each),
   trimmed and boned

½ cup all-purpose flour

¼ teaspoon paprika

Black pepper to taste

¼ cup egg substitute

2 tablespoons low-fat
   nondairy margarine

8 thin tomato slices

¼ cup minced onion

½ cup sliced mushrooms

¼ cup reduced-fat
   mayonnaise

The tantalizing flavor will surprise you, since no cheese is used.

1. Preheat the oven to 375°F. Lightly coat a large skillet and a shallow baking pan with nonstick cooking spray.

2. Pound the veal slices flat. In a small bowl, combine the flour, paprika, and black pepper. Pour the egg substitute in a separate small bowl.

3. In a large skillet, melt the margarine over medium heat. Dredge 3 to 4 of the veal slices first in the seasoned flour, then in the egg substitute, and then in the seasoned flour again. Add to the skillet and sauté until browned on both sides. Transfer to the baking pan and repeat with the remaining veal slices. Top the veal slices with the tomato slices.

4. When all the veal has been browned and placed in the baking pan, add the onion to the skillet and sauté until transparent.

5. Add the mushrooms and sauté for 1 minute more.

6. Remove the skillet from the heat and allow the mixture to cool.

7. When the mixture has cooled, blend in the mayonnaise and pour over the veal. Place the pan in the oven and bake until tender, about 30 minutes.

8. Serve with a green or yellow vegetable.

NUTRITIONAL FACTS PER SERVING

Calories: 310	Protein: 23 g	Carbohydrates: 17 g
Calcium: 23 mg	Total Fat: 13 g (38% fat cals)	Saturated Fat: 5 g

---

EXCHANGES, PER SERVING: 3 Lean Meat; 1 Starch; 1 Fat.

Veal Ribs in Cream and Sage Sauce

Sage imparts the special flavor to this veal dish.

Yield: 6 servings
Prep. time: 1 hour 40 min.

1. In a large skillet, melt the margarine over medium heat. Add the veal ribs and sauté until browned on all sides. Remove the ribs from the skillet and drain out most of the fat.

2. Add the onions to the skillet and sauté until soft.

3. Add the flour, then the water; stir. Bring to a boil, stirring constantly.

4. Return the ribs to the skillet and add the garlic. Cover, lower the heat, and simmer until the ribs are tender, about 1 hour.

5. Add the soymilk, bring the mixture to a boil, and reduce the heat.

6. Add the sage and black pepper. Stir.

7. Serve with Spanish rice.

1 tablespoon low-fat
   nondairy margarine

4 pounds veal ribs

1 cup chopped onion

1 tablespoon all-purpose flour

1 cup water

1 tablespoon chopped garlic

1/2 cup nonfat soymilk

1 tablespoon ground sage

Black pepper to taste

NUTRITIONAL FACTS PER SERVING

Calories: 278   Protein: 24 g   Carbohydrates: 3 g
Calcium: 22.6 mg   Total Fat: 12 g (39% fat cals)   Saturated Fat: 4.6 g

---

EXCHANGES, PER SERVING: 3½ Medium Fat Meat.

Veal Stew

Yield: 12 servings
Prep. time: 1 hour 45 min.

3-pound veal roast, trimmed
   and cut into 1-inch cubes

3 cups beef bouillon

2 large onions, cut into
   quarters

3 large carrots, cut into
   1-inch slices

1 cup celery chunks (1-inch
   pieces)

2 tablespoons nondairy
   margarine

2 tablespoons all-purpose
   flour

1 cup nonfat soymilk

2 teaspoons lemon juice

¼ teaspoon chopped
   parsley, as garnish

Serve over brown rice for a hearty winter meal.

1. Lightly coat a large saucepan with nonstick cooking spray. In the saucepan, combine the veal, bouillon, onions, carrots, and celery. Cook over low heat for 1½ hours.

2. In a small saucepan, melt the margarine over low heat. Add the flour and stir until smooth. Add to the veal mixture and simmer for 10 minutes.

3. Add the soymilk and stir briefly. Add the lemon juice and stir.

4. Serve garnished with the parsley.

NUTRITIONAL FACTS PER SERVING

Calories: 220	Protein: 24 g	Carbohydrates: 4 g
Calcium: 20 mg	Total Fat: 11 g (45% fat cals)	Saturated Fat: 4.4 g

---

EXCHANGES, PER SERVING: 3 Lean Meat; 1 Vegetable.

Lamb Souvlaki

A popular, flavorful lamb recipe from the Middle East.

Yield: 8 servings
Prep. time: 1 hour 5 min.

1. Spray a large skillet with nonstick cooking spray. Add the ground lamb and sauté slowly over low heat until lightly browned.

2. Add the onion and garlic, and sauté until the onion is limp.

3. Stir in the tomatoes, bouillon, and oregano. Raise the heat to medium and bring the mixture to a boil. Add the rice, cover the skillet, and simmer until the rice is tender, about 45 minutes.

4. When ready to serve, stir in the lettuce and heat through. Remove the skillet from the heat. Cut the pita breads in half to make pockets. Spoon $\frac{1}{8}$ of the lamb mixture into each pocket and top the filling with $\frac{1}{2}$ tablespoon of the Mock Sour Cream. Serve immediately.

1 pound ground lean lamb roast

1 onion, chopped

$\frac{1}{2}$ teaspoon minced garlic

2 cups stewed tomatoes

$1\frac{1}{2}$ cups chicken bouillon

$\frac{1}{4}$ teaspoon dried oregano

1 cup uncooked brown rice

4 cups chopped lettuce

4 pita breads

$\frac{1}{4}$ cup Mock Sour Cream (see page 62)

NUTRITIONAL FACTS PER SERVING

Calories: 260	Protein: 18 g	Carbohydrates: 17 g
Calcium: 46 mg	Total Fat: 11 g (38% fat cals)	Saturated Fat: 7 g

---

EXCHANGES, PER SERVING: 2 Lean Meat; 1 Starch; 1 Fat.

Lamb Sautéed in Cream

Yield: 5 servings
Prep. time: 1 hour 30 min.

1 tablespoon low-fat
   nondairy margarine

1-pound lean lamb roast,
   cut into 1-inch cubes

¼ cup reduced-lactose skim
   milk

½ teaspoon dried parsley

An unusual but simple recipe for lamb lovers.

1. In a large skillet, melt the margarine over medium heat. Add the lamb and sauté until browned on all sides, about 5 minutes.

2. Cover the skillet, reduce the heat, and simmer until the lamb is tender, about 1 hour.

3. Remove the lamb from the skillet using a slotted spoon, and arrange on a serving platter. Cover to keep warm.

4. Add the milk to the pan juices and simmer until the liquid is reduced to half its original volume.

5. Pour the sauce over the lamb and garnish with the parsley. Serve with rigatoni and asparagus spears.

NUTRITIONAL FACTS PER SERVING

Calories: 180	Protein: 22 g	Carbohydrates: 1 g
Calcium: 24 mg	Total Fat: 9 g (45% fat cals)	Saturated Fat: 5.4 g

---

EXCHANGES, PER SERVING: 3 Lean Meat.

11

Desserts

A bonus of learning to cook with nondairy foods is the discovery that there are so many desserts–from Banana Cream Pie to Chocolate Mousse to Strawberry Ice Cream–that can be made without milk products. This chapter, though the largest in the book, presents just a sampling of the many concoctions possible. Use these recipes and your imagination to make any meal special.

Lemon Sponge Cake

Yield: 10 servings
Prep. time: 25 minutes
Baking time: 40–45 min.

4 eggs, separated

¾ cup sugar

2 tablespoons lemon juice

Rind of 1 lemon, grated

½ cup all-purpose flour

1 teaspoon baking powder

½ teaspoon cream of tartar

Delicious whether simply garnished with fresh berries or used to make an elaborate trifle.

1. Preheat the oven to 325°F. Lightly coat a 10-inch tube pan with nonstick cooking spray.

2. In a large bowl, combine the egg yolks, sugar, lemon juice, and lemon rind. Mix with an electric mixer at medium speed until thick and lemon colored, about 10 minutes.

3. In a small bowl, sift together the flour and baking powder. Add to the egg-yolk mixture and beat with the mixer at low speed for 2 minutes.

4. In a medium bowl, combine the egg whites and cream of tartar. Beat with the mixer at high speed until stiff peaks can be formed. Fold into the egg-yolk mixture.

5. Pour the batter into the tube pan. Place the cake in the oven and bake until the top is golden, about 40 to 45 minutes.

6. Remove the cake from the oven, set on a wire rack, and allow to cool completely before removing from the pan.

NUTRITIONAL FACTS PER SERVING

Calories: 109	Protein: 3 g	Carbohydrates: 15 g
Calcium: 15 mg	Total Fat: 2.5 g (21% fat cals)	Saturated Fat: 0.7 g

EXCHANGES, PER SERVING: 1 Starch; ½ Fat.

Angel Food Cake

Serve with sherbet or flavored ice for a party-time dessert.

Yield: 10 servings
Prep. time: 15 minutes
Baking time: 45 min.

1. Preheat the oven to 375°F. Lightly coat a 10-inch tube pan with nonstick cooking spray.

2. In a large bowl, combine the egg whites and salt. Beat with an electric mixer at high speed until foamy.

3. Add the cream of tartar. Beat until soft peaks form and hold their shape.

4. In a separate bowl, sift together the flour, sugar, and confectioners' sugar. Fold into the egg whites. Fold in the lemon juice.

5. Pour the batter into the tube pan. Place the cake in the oven and bake until a cake tester inserted in the center comes out clean, about 45 minutes.

6. Remove the cake from the oven, set on a wire rack, and allow to cool completely before removing from the pan.

12 egg whites, at room
 temperature

$\frac{1}{4}$ teaspoon salt

1 teaspoon cream of tartar

1$\frac{1}{4}$ cups all-purpose flour

1$\frac{1}{4}$ cups sugar

1 cup confectioners' sugar

1 tablespoon lemon juice

NUTRITIONAL FACTS PER SERVING

Calories: 174	Protein: 5.4 g	Carbohydrates: 37 g
Calcium: 11 mg	Total Fat: 0.7 g (4% fat cals)	Saturated Fat: 0 g

EXCHANGES, PER SERVING: 2$\frac{1}{2}$ Starch.

Variations

Rum Angel Food Cake: Serve each slice with 1 tablespoon of a syrup made by mixing $\frac{1}{2}$ cup water, $\frac{1}{2}$ cup rum, and 1 teaspoon sugar.

Chocolate Angel Food Cake: Replace $\frac{1}{4}$ cup of the flour with $\frac{1}{4}$ cup cocoa powder.

Coffee Cake

Yield: 16 servings
Prep. time: 15 minutes
Baking time: 1 hour

2 cups sugar

½ cup nondairy margarine,
   softened

2 eggs

½ cup egg substitute

3 cups all-purpose flour

3 teaspoons baking powder

1 cup orange juice

2 ounces bittersweet
   chocolate bits

2 teaspoons cinnamon

A great treat with your favorite beverage.

1. Preheat the oven to 350°F. Lightly coat a 13-x-9-inch cake pan with nonstick cooking spray.

2. Set aside 1 tablespoon of the sugar for later use. Combine the remaining sugar with the margarine, eggs, and egg substitute in a blender. Blend until smooth.

3. In a medium bowl, sift together the flour and baking powder. Add alternately with the orange juice to the sugar-margarine mixture and blend. Add the chocolate bits and stir. Pour the batter into the cake pan.

4. In a small bowl, combine the cinnamon with the reserved sugar; mix well. Sprinkle on top of the batter.

5. Place the cake in the oven and bake until a cake tester inserted in the center comes out clean, about 1 hour. Serve warm or cold.

NUTRITIONAL FACTS PER SERVING

Calories: 263	Protein: 4 g	Carbohydrates: 44 g
Calcium: 27 mg	Total Fat: 8 g (27% fat cals)	Saturated Fat: 2 g

---

EXCHANGES, PER SERVING: 3 Starch; 1½ Fat.

Banana Cake

A marvelous way to use ripe bananas.

1. Preheat the oven to 350°F. Lightly coat an 8-inch-square cake pan with nonstick cooking spray.

2. In a large bowl, sift together the flour, baking powder, and baking soda. Add the remaining ingredients and beat with an electric mixer at medium speed until smooth.

3. Pour the batter into the cake pan. Place the cake in the oven and bake until a cake tester inserted in the center comes out clean, about 25 minutes.

4. Remove the cake from the oven, set on a wire rack, and allow to cool completely before serving.

Yield: 16 servings
Prep. time: 20 minutes
Baking time: 25 min.

2 cups all-purpose flour

3 teaspoons baking powder

1 teaspoon baking soda

1½ cups mashed ripe bananas

1 cup sugar

½ cup vegetable oil

2 eggs

¼ cup egg substitute

1 teaspoon vanilla extract

NUTRITIONAL FACTS PER SERVING

Calories: 195	Protein: 2.8 g	Carbohydrates: 29 g
Calcium: 9 mg	Total Fat: 7.8 g (36% fat cals)	Saturated Fat: 1.3 g

EXCHANGES, PER SERVING: 2 Starch; 1½ Fat.

Chocolate Frosting

Yield: 2 cups
Prep. time: 15 minutes

2 cups confectioners' sugar

½ cup nondairy margarine, softened

½ cup egg substitute

½ cup cocoa powder

A creamy frosting to top any cake.

1. In a medium bowl, sift the sugar. Add the margarine and cream until fluffy.

2. Add the egg substitute and beat with a fork until smooth.

3. Sift the cocoa powder and add. Beat well. If the frosting is too thick, add warm water by teaspoonfuls until the desired consistency is reached.

Note: This will frost and fill a 9-inch 2-layer cake.

NUTRITIONAL FACTS PER SERVING

Calories: 156	Protein: 2.4 g	Carbohydrates: 26 g
Calcium: 6.4 mg	Total Fat: 6 g (35% fat cals)	Saturated Fat: 1 g

---

EXCHANGES, PER SERVING (2-X-2-INCH PIECE LAYER CAKE):
1½ Starch; 1 Fat.

Lemon Pie

Yield: 10 servings
Prep. time: 25 minutes

1 cup sugar

¼ cup cornstarch

1 cup water

½ cup lemon juice

2 tablespoons grated lemon rind

2 tablespoons nondairy margarine

1 9-inch Pie Crust, baked (see page 162)

A cool, smooth ending to any meal.

1. In a large saucepan, combine the sugar and cornstarch. Gradually stir in the water. Cook over medium heat, stirring constantly, until the mixture begins to thicken and boil.

2. When the mixture is clear, add the lemon juice, lemon rind, and margarine. Remove the saucepan from the heat and allow the filling to cool slightly. Pour the filling into a medium bowl and place in the refrigerator for at least 1 hour.

3. Spoon the filling into the Pie Crust. Serve chilled.

NUTRITIONAL FACTS PER SERVING

Calories: 161	Protein: 1 g	Carbohydrates: 30 g
Calcium: 1.7 mg	Total Fat: 5.8 g (32% fat cals)	Saturated Fat: 0 g

---

EXCHANGES, PER SERVING: 2 Starch; 1 Fat.

Yogurt Cheesecake

Unusually low in fat but high in taste. This recipe is proof that unconventional ingredients can make mouth-watering desserts.

1. Preheat the oven to 325°F. Lightly coat a 9-inch-square cake pan with nonstick cooking spray.

2. In a large bowl, combine the yogurt cheese with the sugar, cornstarch, vanilla, and lemon juice. Blend well. Stir in the eggs.

3. Spoon the batter into the cake pan. Place the cake in the oven and bake until the center is set, about 25 minutes.

4. Remove the cake from the oven, set on a wire rack, and allow to cool slightly. Place in the refrigerator for at least 1 hour. Serve chilled.

Yield: 8 servings
Prep. time: 10 minutes
Baking time: 25 min.

Cheese obtained from filtering 32 ounces of nonpasteurized low-fat plain yogurt (see below)

2 tablespoons sugar

1 tablespoon cornstarch

2 teaspoons vanilla extract

1 teaspoon lemon juice

2 eggs, beaten

NUTRITIONAL FACTS PER SERVING

Calories: 91	Protein: 7.5 g	Carbohydrates: 12 g
Calcium: 231 mg	Total Fat: 1.4 g (14% fat cals)	Saturated Fat: 0.5 g

EXCHANGES, PER SERVING: 1 Milk; ½ Fat.

Yogurt Cheese

Yogurt cheese is a homemade product that can be used in place of cottage cheese, cream cheese, or other soft cheeses. It is well tolerated by lactase-deficient individuals because the yogurt cultures produce the lacking enzyme. If possible, use yogurt that was not pasteurized to make yogurt cheese because pasteurization inactivates the enzyme. Nonpasteurized yogurts are made by Dannon, Columbo, Yoplait, Kraft, and Breyers.

The equipment required to make yogurt cheese is minimal. You will need either a funnel-shaped yogurt strainer, available in gourmet food stores, or several layers of 8-x-10-inch gauze sheets, folded into a funnel-shaped bag. You will also need a container to catch the liquid that drains from the yogurt. To strain 32 ounces of yogurt, use a 16-ounce glass jar.

To make yogurt cheese, fill your strainer with the yogurt and suspend it over the jar. (If you are using a gauze bag, you might find a kebab skewer helpful.) Then place the jar in the refrigerator for twelve hours. The liquid that separates from the yogurt will collect in the jar, while the cheeselike yogurt solids—the yogurt cheese—will remain in the filter.

Yogurt cheese can be used as a low-lactose cheese substitute in some recipes. As with any recipe in which you plan to substitute a low-lactose product for a regular dairy item, experiment before whipping up the dish for company. Or become more familiar with this ingredient by first making Yogurt Cheesecake (above) and Strawberry Ice Cream (page 175).

Yogurt cheese is easy to make and delicious. It is well worth the effort.

Tofu Cheesecake

Yield: 12 servings
Prep. time: 15 minutes
Baking time: 40 min.

2 eggs

2 egg whites

8 ounces soft tofu,
   squeezed dry and cut
   into 1-inch cubes

¼ cup maple syrup

2 tablespoons lemon juice

2 teaspoons vanilla extract

4 ounces nondairy cream
   cheese

1 9-inch Graham Cracker
   Crust (see page 162)

2 cups sliced raspberries

Really tastes like cheesecake but contains no dairy products.

1. Preheat the oven to 350°F.

2. In a food processor, combine the eggs and egg whites. Whip for 3 to 4 seconds.

3. Add the tofu, maple syrup, lemon juice, and vanilla extract. Blend until smooth.

4. Add the cream cheese a little at a time, blending until smooth.

5. Spoon the filling into the Graham Cracker Crust. Place the pie in the oven and bake until the center is set, about 40 minutes.

6. Remove the pie from the oven, set on a wire rack, and allow to cool slightly. Top with the raspberries and place in the refrigerator for at least 1 hour. Serve chilled.

NUTRITIONAL FACTS PER SERVING

Calories: 152	Protein: 4.5 g	Carbohydrates: 18 g
Calcium: 49.5 mg	Total Fat: 7 g (41% fat cals)	Saturated Fat: 2.5 g

---

EXCHANGES, PER SERVING: 1 Starch; 1 Fat.

Orange Tofu Cheesecake

The orange renders an uncommon but delightful flavor to this "cheesecake."

1. Preheat the oven to 350°F.

2. In a large bowl, combine the tofu, honey, orange juice, oil, orange peel, and vanilla extract. Blend with an electric mixer at low speed until smooth, about 30 to 40 seconds.

3. Spoon the filling into the Graham Cracker Crust. Place the pie in the oven and bake until the center is set, about 1 hour.

4. Remove the pie from the oven, set on a wire rack, and allow to cool slightly. Place in the refrigerator for at least 1 hour.

5. Serve well chilled, garnished with drained crushed pineapple or sliced strawberries.

Yield: 12 servings
Prep. time: 5 minutes
Baking time: 1 hour

20 ounces soft tofu, squeezed dry and cut into 1-inch cubes

½ cup honey

3 tablespoons orange juice

2 tablespoons oil

2 tablespoons grated orange peel

2 teaspoons vanilla extract

1 9-inch Graham Cracker Crust (see page 162)

NUTRITIONAL FACTS PER SERVING

Calories: 250	Protein: 4.5 g	Carbohydrates: 29 g
Calcium: 62 mg	Total Fat: 9 g (32% fat cals)	Saturated Fat: 1.7 g

EXCHANGES, PER SERVING: 2 Starch; 2 Fat.

Pumpkin Pie

Yield: 10 servings
Prep. time: 15 minutes
Baking time: 35–45 min.

2 cups canned pumpkin

1½ cups water

⅔ cup firmly packed brown
sugar

6 tablespoons cornstarch

1 tablespoon pumpkin pie
spice

1 9-inch Pie Crust, unbaked
(see page 162)

½ cup brown sugar

You will not feel deprived on Thanksgiving with this reduced-fat treat.

1. Preheat the oven to 425°F.

2. In a large saucepan, combine the pumpkin, water, ⅔ cup brown sugar, cornstarch, and pumpkin pie spice. Cook over low heat, stirring constantly, until the mixture begins to thicken.

3. Spoon the filling into the Pie Crust. Place the pie in the oven and bake for 15 minutes. Reduce the temperature to 350°F and bake until the filling is set, about 20 to 30 minutes more.

4. Sprinkle the ½ cup brown sugar over the top of the pie and bake for an additional 5 minutes.

5. Remove the pie from the oven and allow to cool completely before serving.

NUTRITIONAL FACTS PER SERVING

Calories: 201	Protein: 1.5 g	Carbohydrates: 44 g
Calcium: 35 mg	Total Fat: 4.8 g (21% fat cals)	Saturated Fat: 0 g

---

EXCHANGES, PER SERVING: 3 Starch; 1 Fat.

Apricot Cream Pie

No one can refuse a slice of this unique pie.

1. In a small bowl, soften the gelatin powder in the cold water.

2. Using a blender, food processor, or food mill, purée the dried apricots until they are the consistency of a smooth paste. Add a little water if necessary to ensure a smooth consistency.

3. In a large saucepan, combine the apricot purée, apricot nectar, sugar, and lemon juice. Heat over low heat, stirring constantly, until the sugar is dissolved.

4. Add the softened gelatin and stir until dissolved.

5. Remove the saucepan from the heat and allow the mixture to cool slightly. Pour the mixture into a large bowl and place in the refrigerator until partially set.

6. Whip the chilled mixture with a wire whisk until fluffy, then fold in the whipped topping. Spoon into the Pie Crust and place in the refrigerator. Serve chilled.

Yield: 10 servings
Prep. time: 25 minutes

1 envelope unflavored gelatin powder

$\frac{1}{4}$ cup cold water

8 dried apricots

$\frac{1}{2}$ cup apricot nectar

$\frac{1}{3}$ cup sugar

1 tablespoon lemon juice

1 cup nondairy whipped topping

1 9-inch Pie Crust, baked (see page 162)

NUTRITIONAL FACTS PER SERVING

Calories: 205	Protein: 2 g	Carbohydrates: 28 g
Calcium: 5.2 mg	Total Fat: 5.4 g (24% fat cals)	Saturated Fat: 2 g

EXCHANGES, PER SERVING: 2 Starch; 1 Fat.

Banana Cream Pie

Yield: 10 servings
Prep. time: 15 minutes

3 medium bananas

6 ounces soft tofu,
    squeezed dry

2 tablespoons oil

2 tablespoons honey

1 tablespoon reduced-fat
    soymilk

1 teaspoon lemon juice

$\frac{1}{2}$ teaspoon vanilla extract

$\frac{1}{4}$ teaspoon cinnamon

1 9-inch Pie Crust, baked
    (see page 162)

One of the more popular desserts.

1. Set aside 1 banana for later use. Cut the remaining bananas into 1-inch chunks.

2. In a blender, combine the banana chunks, tofu, oil, honey, soymilk, lemon juice, vanilla extract, and cinnamon. Blend until smooth.

3. Cut the reserved banana into $\frac{1}{4}$-inch slices. Arrange most of the slices to cover the bottom of the Pie Crust, then dip the leftovers in lemon juice to prevent browning. Set the leftovers aside.

4. Spoon the filling into the Pie Crust. Decorate the top of the pie with a few of the leftover banana slices and place the pie in the refrigerator for at least 1 hour. Serve chilled.

NUTRITIONAL FACTS PER SERVING

Calories: 178	Protein: 3.2 g	Carbohydrates: 22 g
Calcium: 19 mg	Total Fat: 7.6 g (38% fat cals)	Saturated Fat: 0.6 g

---

EXCHANGES, PER SERVING: $\frac{1}{2}$ Fruit; 1 Starch; $1\frac{1}{2}$ Fat.

Chocolate Cream Pie

A good, chocolatey substitute for the one made with milk.

1. In a small bowl, soften the gelatin powder in the cold water.

2. In a medium bowl, beat the egg yolks until thick. Add the cognac, vanilla extract, and $\frac{1}{2}$ cup of the sugar, and beat again.

3. In a small saucepan, melt the margarine over very low heat. Add the water and cocoa powder, and stir until well blended. Add the softened gelatin and stir until dissolved. Add the cocoa mixture to the egg-yolk mixture and beat. Place in the refrigerator until almost set.

4. In a large bowl, beat the egg whites with an electric mixer at medium speed until stiff but not dry. Gradually add the remaining sugar, continuing to beat. Fold in the cocoa mixture.

5. Spoon the filling into the Graham Cracker Crust and place in the refrigerator for at least 1 hour. Serve chilled.

Yield: 10 servings
Prep. time: 40 minutes

1 envelope unflavored gelatin powder

$\frac{1}{4}$ cup cold water

3 eggs, separated, at room temperature

2 tablespoons cognac

1 teaspoon vanilla extract

1 cup sugar

2 tablespoons nondairy margarine

$\frac{1}{2}$ cup water

6 tablespoons cocoa powder

1 9-inch Graham Cracker Crust, baked (see page 162)

NUTRITIONAL FACTS PER SERVING

Calories: 230	Protein: 4 g	Carbohydrates: 33 g
Calcium: 51 mg	Total Fat: 8 g (31% fat cals)	Saturated Fat: 1 g

EXCHANGES, PER SERVING: 2 Starch; $1\frac{1}{2}$ Fat.

Pie Crust

Yield: Two 9-inch pie crusts
Prep. time: 1 hour
Baking time: 0–8 min.

2 cups all-purpose flour

⅔ cup nondairy margarine

4–5 tablespoons cold water

Easy to prepare.

1. In a medium bowl, combine the flour and margarine. Mix with a pastry blender or 2 knives until coarse in texture. Add the water 1 tablespoon at a time, blending thoroughly. Place the dough in the refrigerator for at least 1 hour.

2. Remove the dough from the refrigerator. Turn it out onto a floured surface and divide it in half. Roll out 1 half to an 11-inch diameter and place in a nonstick 9-inch pie pan. Prick with a fork. Repeat with the remaining piece of dough.

3. If your recipe calls for a baked pie crust, place the pie shell in a preheated 425°F oven and bake for 8 minutes or until lightly browned. If your recipe calls for an unbaked pie shell, just fill the shell and bake according to your pie recipe.

NUTRITIONAL FACTS PER SERVING
See specific pie recipe.

EXCHANGES: See specific pie recipe.

Graham Cracker Crust

Yield: One 9-inch pie crust
Prep. time: 5 minutes

1 cup fine graham cracker crumbs

¼ cup nondairy margarine, melted

1 teaspoon sugar

Simple, quick, and popular.

1. In a small bowl, combine all the ingredients. Mix well.

2. Press the mixture into a nonstick 9-inch pie pan.

3. If your recipe calls for a baked pie crust, place the pie shell in a preheated 350°F oven and bake for 10 minutes. If your recipe calls for an unbaked pie shell, just fill the shell and bake according to your pie recipe.

NUTRITIONAL FACTS PER SERVING
See specific pie recipe.

EXCHANGES: See specific pie recipe.

Rice Pudding

A pleasant way to serve the most widely used grain in the world.

1. Preheat the oven to 375°F. Lightly coat 6 custard cups with nonstick cooking spray.

2. In a medium bowl, combine the rice, sugar, margarine, and vanilla extract. Mix well. Fold in the beaten eggs.

3. Divide the pudding evenly among the 6 custard cups. Place the custard cups in the oven and bake until set, about 15 minutes.

4. Top each pudding with 1 teaspoon of the cream and a sprinkling of the cinnamon. Serve warm, or refrigerate and serve cold.

Yield: 6 servings
Prep. time: 10 minutes
Baking time: 15 min.

3 cups cooked white rice

¼ cup sugar

2 tablespoons nondairy margarine

½ teaspoon vanilla extract

2 eggs, beaten

2 tablespoons nondairy cream

⅛ teaspoon cinnamon

NUTRITIONAL FACTS PER SERVING

Calories: 165	Protein: 2.7 g	Carbohydrates: 23 g
Calcium: 14 mg	Total Fat: 4.6 g (25% fat cals)	Saturated Fat: 1 g

EXCHANGES, PER SERVING: 1½ Starch; 1 Fat.

Tapioca Pudding

An especially light finish to a fish meal.

1. In a small saucepan, sprinkle the tapioca. Slowly add the milk, stirring constantly. Add the egg substitute and sugar. Heat over very low heat, stirring constantly, until the mixture begins to boil, about 10 to 12 minutes.

2. Stir in the vanilla extract and spoon into 2 custard cups. Serve warm, or refrigerate and serve cold.

Yield: 2 servings
Prep. time: 20 minutes

1½ tablespoons quick-cooking tapioca

1¼ cups reduced-lactose skim milk

¼ cup egg substitute

3 tablespoons sugar

½ teaspoon vanilla extract

NUTRITIONAL FACTS PER SERVING

Calories: 175	Protein: 9.5 g	Carbohydrates: 26 g
Calcium: 207 mg	Total Fat: 1.5 g (8% fat cals)	Saturated Fat: 0 g

EXCHANGES, PER SERVING: 1 Starch; 1 Milk.

Custard Pudding

Yield: 4 servings
Prep. time: 5 minutes

2 cups reduced-fat soymilk

1 tablespoon honey

1 teaspoon vanilla extract

1½ tablespoons cornstarch

An appetizing dessert that can be enhanced by garnishing with fruit.

1. In a small saucepan, combine the soymilk, honey, and vanilla extract. Place the pan over low heat and stir in the cornstarch. Heat, stirring constantly, until the pudding begins to boil, about 3 to 4 minutes.

2. Spoon the pudding into 4 custard cups and place in the refrigerator for at least 1 hour. Serve chilled.

NUTRITIONAL FACTS PER SERVING

Calories: 82	Protein: 4 g	Carbohydrates: 14 g
Calcium: 28 mg	Total Fat: 2 g (21% fat cals)	Saturated Fat: 0 g

EXCHANGES, PER SERVING: 1 Starch.

Orange Bread Pudding

Yield: 6 servings
Prep. time: 10 minutes
Baking time: 1 hour

2 cups dry dairy-free bread cubes

4 cups reduced-fat soymilk

3 tablespoons nondairy margarine

½ cup sugar

2 eggs, beaten

1 teaspoon cinnamon

1 teaspoon ground nutmeg

Rind of 1 orange, grated

A highly flavored dessert and a choice way to use stale bread.

1. Preheat the oven to 375°F. Lightly coat an 8-inch-square baking pan with nonstick cooking spray.

2. Place the bread cubes in a large bowl.

3. In a medium saucepan, combine the soymilk and margarine. Heat over low heat until the margarine has melted. Pour over the bread cubes and let stand for 3 minutes.

4. Add the sugar, eggs, cinnamon, nutmeg, and orange rind. Mix well.

5. Pour the mixture into the baking pan and set the baking pan in a pan of hot water. Place in the oven and bake until a knife inserted in the center of the pudding comes out clean, about 1 hour. Serve hot, or refrigerate and serve cold.

NUTRITIONAL FACTS PER SERVING

Calories: 295	Protein: 5 g	Carbohydrates: 36 g
Calcium: 75 mg	Total Fat: 9 g (27% fat cals)	Saturated Fat: 1.2 g

EXCHANGES, PER SERVING: 2 Starch; ½ Milk; 2 Fat.

Fruit Mousse

A tasty, light, and healthy dessert.

1. In a blender, combine the bananas, orange, kiwi, and strawberries; blend. Add the yogurt and sugar. Blend until smooth.

2. In a small bowl, soften the gelatin powder in the cold water. Add the boiling water and stir until the gelatin is dissolved. Add to the fruit and blend well.

3. Pour the mousse into 6 parfait glasses and place in the refrigerator for at least 1 hour. Serve chilled.

Yield: 6 servings
Prep. time: 20 minutes

2 ripe bananas, peeled and cut into 1-inch chunks

1 whole orange, peeled and sectioned

1 whole kiwi, peeled and cut into quarters

1 cup frozen strawberries, partially thawed

1 cup nonpasteurized fat-free plain yogurt

3 tablespoons sugar

1 envelope unflavored gelatin powder

¼ cup cold water

¼ cup boiling water

NUTRITIONAL FACTS PER SERVING

Calories: 105	Protein: 3 g	Carbohydrates: 23 g
Calcium: 82 mg	Total Fat: 1 g (9% fat cals)	Saturated Fat: 0 g

---

EXCHANGES, PER SERVING: $1\frac{1}{2}$ Fruit.

Chocolate Mousse

Yield: 8 servings
Prep. time: 30 minutes

1 tablespoon instant coffee
 powder

1 tablespoon boiling water

4 ounces semisweet
 chocolate

3 egg whites

2 egg yolks

¼ cup sugar

2 tablespoons brandy

A delicate, sweet dessert that uses no dairy products.

1. In a small saucepan, dissolve the coffee powder in the boiling water. Add the chocolate, place the pan over very low heat, and melt the chocolate slowly. Remove the pan from the heat and allow the mixture to cool.

2. In a medium bowl, beat the egg whites until stiff but not dry.

3. In a separate bowl, beat the egg yolks until thick. Add the sugar and beat until dissolved. Add the cooled chocolate mixture and the brandy. Stir well. Fold into the egg-white mixture.

4. Pour the mousse into 8 parfait glasses and place in the refrigerator for at least 1 hour. Serve chilled.

NUTRITIONAL FACTS PER SERVING

Calories: 128   Protein: 2 g   Carbohydrates: 14 g
Calcium: 11 mg   Total Fat: 6 g (42% fat cals)   Saturated Fat: 3 g

EXCHANGES, PER SERVING: 1 Starch; 1 Fat.

Fruit Crisp

A delicious low-fat way to meet part of your daily fruit requirement.

1. Preheat the oven to 350°F. Lightly coat an 8-inch-square glass baking dish with nonstick cooking spray.

2. In a small bowl, combine the oats, $\frac{1}{4}$ cup of the brown sugar, the margarine, and $\frac{1}{4}$ teaspoon of the cinnamon. Mix.

3. In the baking dish, combine the remaining brown sugar and cinnamon with the apples, apricots, orange juice, and flour. Mix thoroughly. Sprinkle the oat mixture over the top.

4. Place the dish in the oven and bake for 45 minutes or until lightly browned.

5. Serve hot, or refrigerate and serve cold.

Yield: 10 servings
Prep. time: 5 minutes
Baking time: 45 min.

$\frac{3}{4}$ cup rolled oats

$\frac{1}{2}$ cup brown sugar

4 teaspoons nondairy margarine, melted

$\frac{3}{4}$ teaspoon cinnamon

4 cups thinly sliced peeled apples

2 cups dried apricots, finely chopped

$\frac{1}{4}$ cup orange juice

2 tablespoons all-purpose flour

NUTRITIONAL FACTS PER SERVING

Calories: 140	Protein: 2.4 g	Carbohydrates: 30 g
Calcium: 26 mg	Total Fat: 1.7 g (11% fat cals)	Saturated Fat: 0.3 g

EXCHANGES, PER SERVING: 2 Fruit.

Stewed Figs

Figs are both flavorful and a good source of minerals.

1. The night before, combine the figs, wine, and water in a large saucepan. Let stand overnight.

2. Add the sugar and lemon juice to the figs; stir. Place the saucepan over medium heat and bring the mixture to a boil. Reduce the heat and simmer until the figs are tender, about 15 minutes.

3. Add the cinnamon and stir. Spoon the mixture into a serving bowl and place in the refrigerator for at least 1 hour. Serve cold.

Yield: 6 servings
Prep. time: 20 minutes

1 pound dried figs

1 cup dry white wine

1 cup water

$\frac{1}{4}$ cup sugar

1 tablespoon lemon juice

$\frac{1}{8}$ teaspoon cinnamon

NUTRITIONAL FACTS PER SERVING

Calories: 154	Protein: 1 g	Carbohydrates: 34 g
Calcium: 56 mg	Total Fat: 0.6 g (4% fat cals)	Saturated Fat: 0 g

EXCHANGES, PER SERVING: 2 Fruit.

Mandarin Orange Bavarian

Yield: 4 servings
Prep. time: 15 minutes

3-ounce package orange gelatin powder

11-ounce can mandarin oranges, drained, liquid reserved

2 cups nondairy whipped topping

Children love this dessert.

1. In a large bowl, prepare the orange gelatin according to the package directions. Use the liquid reserved from the mandarin oranges in place of some of the required water. Set aside and allow to cool.

2. When the gelatin is syrupy and partially set, fold in the mandarin oranges, then the whipped topping. Serve cold.

NUTRITIONAL FACTS PER SERVING

Calories: 183	Protein: 2.4 g	Carbohydrates: 34 g
Calcium: 9 mg	Total Fat: 8 g (39% fat cals)	Saturated Fat: 6 g

EXCHANGES, PER SERVING: 2 Fruit; 1½ Fat.

Oatmeal Cookies

Yield: 48 cookies
Prep. time: 10 minutes
Baking time: 10 min.

1 cup sugar

1 cup firmly packed brown sugar

½ cup nondairy margarine, softened

1 teaspoon vanilla extract

1 cup all-purpose flour

4 teaspoons baking powder

¾ cup orange juice

3 cups rolled oats

½ cup chopped walnuts

Chewy morsels that are always in demand.

1. Preheat the oven to 350°F.

2. In a large bowl, combine the sugar, brown sugar, margarine, and vanilla extract. Mix well.

3. In a small bowl, sift together the flour and baking powder. Add alternately with the orange juice to the sugar mixture and stir. Add the oats and walnuts; mix well.

4. Drop the dough by teaspoonfuls onto a nonstick cookie sheet. Place in the oven and bake until the cookies are lightly browned, about 10 minutes.

5. Remove the cookies from the oven and immediately transfer to a wire rack. Allow to cool before serving.

NUTRITIONAL FACTS PER COOKIE

Calories: 110	Protein: 3.3 g	Carbohydrates: 19 g
Calcium: 16 mg	Total Fat: 2.4 g (20% fat cals)	Saturated Fat: 0.2 g

EXCHANGES, PER COOKIE: 1 Starch; ½ Fat.

Prune Whip

A low-fat, airy dessert.

1. In a medium bowl, combine the prune filling with the sugar. Blend well. Fold in 1 cup of the whipped topping.

2. Serve garnished with the remaining whipped topping.

Yield: 8 servings
Prep. time: 5 minutes

1-pound can prune filling

½ cup sugar

2 cups reduced-fat nondairy whipped topping

NUTRITIONAL FACTS PER SERVING

Calories: 190   Protein: 1 g   Carbohydrates: 30 g
Calcium: 21.5 mg   Total Fat: 4.2 g (19% fat cals)   Saturated Fat: 3 g

EXCHANGES, PER SERVING: 1 Starch; 1 Fruit; 1 Fat.

Date-Nut Cookies

A rich-tasting cookie.

1. In a medium bowl, combine the egg and egg substitute; beat until thick. Add the brown sugar and vanilla extract, and stir. Add the peanut butter and dates; mix well. Place the dough in the refrigerator for at least 2 hours.

2. Preheat the oven to 300°F.

3. Drop the dough by teaspoonfuls onto a nonstick cookie sheet. Flatten each mound of dough with a fork. Place in the oven and bake until the cookies are lightly browned, about 25 minutes.

4. Remove the cookies from the oven and immediately transfer to a wire rack. Allow to cool before serving.

Yield: 24 cookies
Prep. time: 10 minutes
Baking time: 25 min.

1 egg

½ cup egg substitute

2 cups brown sugar

1 teaspoon vanilla extract

¾ cup chunky peanut butter

½ cup chopped dates

NUTRITIONAL FACTS PER COOKIE

Calories: 165   Protein: 2.7 g   Carbohydrates: 22 g
Calcium: 26 mg   Total Fat: 4 g (21% fat cals)   Saturated Fat: 0.7 g

EXCHANGES, PER COOKIE: 1½ Starch; 1 Fat.

Macaroons

Yield: 18 cookies
Prep. time: 15 minutes
Baking time: 15 min.

1 cup finely ground almonds

¾ cup sugar

2 egg whites

2 tablespoons cornstarch

2 teaspoons water

Best when fresh out of the oven.

1. Preheat the oven to 375°F. Line a cookie sheet with foil.

2. In a blender, combine the ground almonds and sugar. Add the egg whites, first reserving about 1 tablespoon for later use. Blend for 1 minute.

3. Add the cornstarch and blend, then add the water and blend.

4. Drop the dough by teaspoonfuls onto the cookie sheet, leaving about 3 inches between each cookie. Brush the tops with the reserved egg white. Place in the oven and bake until browned, about 15 minutes.

5. Remove the cookies from the oven and allow to cool for 3 to 4 minutes before removing from the foil. Serve warm or cold.

NUTRITIONAL FACTS PER COOKIE

Calories: 125	Protein: 2.3 g	Carbohydrates: 12 g
Calcium: 35 mg	Total Fat: 6.4 g (46% fat cals)	Saturated Fat: 0.6 g

---

EXCHANGES, PER COOKIE: 1 Starch; 1 Fat.

Fudge Brownies

Perfect for the chocolate lover.

1. Preheat the oven to 325°F. Lightly coat a 9-inch-square baking pan with nonstick cooking spray.

2. In a medium bowl, sift together the cocoa powder, flour, and baking powder. Add the sugar and blend. Stir in the melted margarine.

3. Add the egg substitute and vanilla extract. Beat with an electric mixer until smooth.

4. Spoon the batter into the baking pan and sprinkle with the walnuts. Place in the oven and bake until a cake tester inserted in the center comes out clean, about 20 minutes.

5. Remove the brownies from the oven, set on a wire rack, and allow to cool. Cut into 24 squares and serve.

Yield: 24 servings
Prep. time: 15 minutes
Baking time: 20 min.

½ cup unsweetened cocoa powder

1 cup all-purpose flour

½ teaspoon baking powder

1 cup sugar

½ cup nondairy margarine, melted

½ cup egg substitute

1 teaspoon vanilla extract

2 tablespoons chopped walnuts

NUTRITIONAL FACTS PER SERVING

Calories: 125	Protein: 1 g	Carbohydrates: 14 g
Calcium: 9 mg	Total Fat: 5.6 g (40% fat cals)	Saturated Fat: 1.4 g

EXCHANGES, PER SERVING: 1 Starch; 1 Fat.

Chocolate Low-Fat Brownies

Yield: 16 servings
Prep. time: 20 minutes
Baking time: 30 min.

½ cup plus 1 tablespoon
  cake flour

⅓ cup unsweetened cocoa
  powder

⅛ teaspoon salt

1 medium egg

¼ cup egg substitute

¾ cup sugar

½ cup plain applesauce
  (not the chunky variety)

2 tablespoons oil

2 teaspoons vanilla extract

1 tablespoon powdered
  sugar

These delicious brownies highlight the use of puréed fruits as a fat substitute.

1. Preheat the oven to 350°F. Lightly coat a 9-inch-square baking pan with nonstick cooking spray.

2. In a small bowl, blend together the flour, cocoa, and salt.

3. In a large bowl, use a fork to mix together the egg, egg substitute, sugar, applesauce, oil, and vanilla.

4. Blend the flour mixture into the egg mixture.

5. Spoon the batter into the baking pan. Place the pan in the oven and bake until a cake tester inserted in the center comes out clean, about 30 minutes.

6. Remove the brownies from the oven, set on a wire rack, and cool for 10 minutes. Sprinkle with the powdered sugar, cut into 16 squares, and serve.

NUTRITIONAL FACTS PER SERVING

Calories: 65	Protein: 1.7 g	Carbohydrates: 7.5 g
Calcium: 28 mg	Total Fat: 2.6 g (37% fat cals)	Saturated Fat: 0 g

---

EXCHANGES, PER SERVING: ½ Starch; ½ Fat.

Chocolate Fudge

Surprise your guests at the holidays with this nondairy fudge.

1. In a large heavy saucepan, heat the soymilk over low heat. Add the chocolate and heat until melted. Add the sugar and corn syrup, and heat, stirring constantly, until the sugar is dissolved.

2. Attach a candy thermometer to the saucepan and cook until the mixture reaches the soft ball stage (234°F to 240°F). Remove the pan from the heat and add the margarine and vanilla. Allow to cool to 100°F.

3. Once the mixture has cooled, beat it well with an electric mixer for about 15 seconds. Pour it into an 8-inch-square baking pan and allow to harden.

4. When the fudge has hardened, cut it into 16 squares and serve.

Yield: 16 pieces
Prep. time: 20 minutes

1 ¼ cups reduced-fat soymilk

4 ounces unsweetened chocolate

4 cups sugar

2 tablespoons corn syrup

1 tablespoon nondairy margarine

2 teaspoons vanilla extract

NUTRITIONAL FACTS PER SERVING

Calories: 325	Protein: 1.4 g	Carbohydrates: 52 g
Calcium: 10 mg	Total Fat: 4.7 g (13% fat cals)	Saturated Fat: 2 g

EXCHANGES, PER SERVING: 3½ Starch; 1 Fat.

Orange Ice

Easier to make than sherbet, but not quite as creamy.

1. In a large saucepan, combine the water and sugar. Boil for 5 minutes. Add the orange juice, lemon juice, and orange rind, and stir. Remove the pan from the heat and allow the mixture to cool.

2. Strain the mixture. Pour into a freezer tray and freeze until firm.

Yield: 8 servings
Prep. time: 10 minutes
plus freezing time

4 cups water

2 cups sugar

2 cups orange juice

¼ cup lemon juice

Rinds of 2 oranges, grated

NUTRITIONAL FACTS PER SERVING

Calories: 270	Protein: 0.4 g	Carbohydrates: 54.5 g
Calcium: 6.7 mg	Total Fat: 0 g (0% fat cals)	Saturated Fat: 0 g

EXCHANGES, PER SERVING: 3 Starch; ½ Fruit.

Lime Sherbet

Yield: 6 servings
Prep. time: 15 minutes
plus freezing time

2 egg whites

2 cups soymilk

1 cup light corn syrup

¾ cup lime juice

¼ cup sugar

Rinds of 3 limes, grated

Truly refreshing between courses or as dessert.

1. In a medium bowl, beat the egg whites with an electric mixer or egg beater until stiff but not dry. Add the remaining ingredients, continuing to beat. Pour into a freezer tray and freeze until firm, about 1 hour.

2. Transfer the sherbet to a chilled large bowl and beat until creamy. Return to the freezer tray and freeze again until firm, about 1 hour.

NUTRITIONAL FACTS PER SERVING

Calories: 270   Protein: 4 g   Carbohydrates: 52 g
Calcium: 22 mg   Total Fat: 1.3 g (4% fat cals)   Saturated Fat: 0 g

---

EXCHANGES, PER SERVING: 3 Starch; ½ Fruit.

Apricot Sherbet

Yield: 6 servings
Prep. time: 20 minutes
plus freezing time

1 envelope unflavored
   gelatin powder

½ cup cold water

3 cups apricot nectar

¾ cup light corn syrup

¼ cup lemon juice

Takes a little time, but the result is a flavorful, fat-free dessert.

1. In a large saucepan, sprinkle the gelatin powder onto the water. Heat over low heat, stirring constantly, until the gelatin is dissolved. Stir in the remaining ingredients. Pour into a freezer tray and freeze until firm, about 1 hour.

2. Transfer the sherbet to a chilled large bowl and beat with an electric mixer or egg beater until light and creamy. Return to the freezer tray and freeze again until firm, about 3 to 4 hours.

NUTRITIONAL FACTS PER SERVING

Calories: 220   Protein: 1 g   Carbohydrates: 48 g
Calcium: 8.5 mg   Total Fat: 0 g (0% fat cals)   Saturated Fat: 0 g

---

EXCHANGES, PER SERVING: 2 Starch; 1 Fruit.

Chocolate Ice Cream

Satisfies the sweet tooth.

Yield: 6 servings
Prep. time: 10 minutes
plus freezing time

1. In a large bowl, beat the egg whites with an electric mixer or egg beater until stiff but not dry. Add the sugar, continuing to beat. Fold in the whipped topping. Add the chocolate syrup and vanilla extract, and gently stir.

2. Spoon the mixture into a 1-pint plastic container. Place in the freezer until firm, about 1 hour.

6 egg whites

¾ cup sugar

2 cups nondairy whipped topping

3 tablespoons nondairy chocolate syrup

2 teaspoons vanilla extract

NUTRITIONAL FACTS PER SERVING

Calories: 183	Protein: 7 g	Carbohydrates: 34 g
Calcium: 5 mg	Total Fat: 4 g (19% fat cals)	Saturated Fat: 3 g

EXCHANGES, PER SERVING: ½ Very Lean Meat; 2 Starch.

Strawberry Ice Cream

With strawberries easily available, you can always enjoy this treat.

Yield: 6 servings
Prep. time: 15 minutes
plus freezing time

1. In a large bowl, combine the yogurt cheese and strawberries. Blend lightly. Pour the mixture into a freezer tray and freeze until firm.

2. Transfer the mixture to a chilled large bowl and break into pieces. Beat with an electric mixer or egg beater until smooth. Spoon into a chilled mold and freeze again until firm, about 1 hour.

Cheese obtained from filtering 32 ounces of nonpasteurized plain yogurt (see page 155)

2 pints strawberries, washed, hulled, and crushed

NUTRITIONAL FACTS PER SERVING

Calories: 111	Protein: 8 g	Carbohydrates: 14 g
Calcium: 273 mg	Total Fat: 2.5 g (20% fat cals)	Saturated Fat: 1.6 g

EXCHANGES, PER SERVING: 1 Milk; ½ Fat.

Vanilla Ice Cream

Yield: 8 servings
Prep. time: 20 minutes
plus freezing time

1 cup nondairy whipped
   topping

½ cup sugar

1 teaspoon vanilla extract

1 egg, separated, at room
   temperature

Serve with melon balls for a special presentation.

1. In a medium bowl, combine the whipped topping, sugar, vanilla extract, and egg yolk; blend well. Place in the freezer for 30 minutes.

2. In a small bowl, beat the egg white with an electric mixer or egg beater until stiff but not dry.

3. Remove the frozen mixture from the freezer and fold in the egg white. Blend gently for 1 minute. Pour into a plastic container. Place in the freezer until firm, about 1 hour.

NUTRITIONAL FACTS PER SERVING

Calories: 81	Protein: 0.9 g	Carbohydrates: 13 g
Calcium: 3.5 mg	Total Fat: 2 g (24% fat cals)	Saturated Fat: 1.5 g

EXCHANGES, PER SERVING: 1 Starch.

12

Beverages

Soymilk, tofu, and nondairy cream help make lactose-free drinks
that are creamy and nutritious. Other favorites are Rice Dream,
a rice-based nondairy beverage produced by Imagine Foods, and Almondmylk,
made by Wholesome and Hearty from rice syrup and almonds.

All the beverages presented in this chapter take just a few seconds
to prepare. In many cases, you can toss in some extra fruit
to add both texture and nutrients to the drink.

Fruit Shake

Yield: 3 servings
Prep. time: 5 minutes

1 cup reduced-fat soymilk

1 banana, cut into 1-inch
  chunks

2 ice cubes

A delightful way to fit bananas into your diet.

1. In a blender, combine all the ingredients. Blend at high speed until smooth.

2. Pour the mixture into 3 tall glasses and serve immediately.

NUTRITIONAL FACTS PER SERVING

Calories: 64   Protein: 1.7 g   Carbohydrates: 13.9 g
Calcium: 22.3 mg   Total Fat: 0.9 g (13% fat cals)   Saturated Fat: 0 g

---

EXCHANGES, PER SERVING: 1 Fruit.

Variations

Substitute 1 cup canned apricots, 2 cups frozen raspberries, or $2\frac{1}{2}$ cups frozen strawberries for the banana.

Creamy Fruit Shake

Yield: 4 servings
Prep. time: 5 minutes

$1\frac{1}{2}$ cups frozen
  strawberries, partially
  thawed

10 ounces soft tofu, drained

1 cup orange juice

4 ice cubes

A thick, flavorful, well-liked drink.

1. In a blender, combine all the ingredients. Blend at high speed until smooth.

2. Pour the mixture into 4 tall glasses and serve immediately.

NUTRITIONAL FACTS PER SERVING

Calories: 83   Protein: 5 g   Carbohydrates: 11 g
Calcium: 86 mg   Total Fat: 2.6 g (28% fat cals)   Saturated Fat: 0.5 g

---

EXCHANGES, PER SERVING: $\frac{1}{2}$ Medium Fat Meat; $\frac{1}{2}$ Fruit.

Hawaiian Shake

Add a sprig of mint for eye appeal.

Yield: 3 servings
Prep. time: 5 minutes

1. In a blender, combine all the ingredients. Blend at high speed until smooth.

2. Pour the mixture into 3 tall glasses and serve immediately.

1 cup reduced-fat soymilk

1 cup unsweetened pineapple juice

4 ice cubes

NUTRITIONAL FACTS PER SERVING

Calories: 64
Calcium: 29 mg

Protein: 1.6 g
Total Fat: 0.7 g (10% fat cals)

Carbohydrates: 12 g
Saturated Fat: 0 g

EXCHANGES, PER SERVING: $\frac{1}{2}$ Fruit.

Variations

Substitute 1 cup orange juice or $\frac{2}{3}$ cup cranberry juice for the pineapple juice.

Coffee Frappé

A wonderful refreshment for coffee aficionados.

Yield: 3 servings
Prep. time: 5 minutes

1. In a blender, combine all the ingredients. Blend at high speed until smooth.

2. Pour the mixture into 3 tall glasses and serve immediately.

1 cup reduced-fat soymilk

1 cup double-strength coffee

$\frac{1}{2}$ teaspoon sugar

4 ice cubes

NUTRITIONAL FACTS PER SERVING

Calories: 33
Calcium: 18 mg

Protein: 1.6 g
Total Fat: 0.7 g (19% fat cals)

Carbohydrates: 4 g
Saturated Fat: 0 g

EXCHANGES, PER SERVING: FREE.

Chocolate Shake

Yield: 1 serving
Prep. time: 5 minutes

6 ounces reduced-fat soymilk

2 heaping teaspoons instant nondairy chocolate drink mix

¼ teaspoon vanilla extract

4 ice cubes

A creamy, satisfying beverage.

1. In a blender, combine all the ingredients. Blend at high speed until smooth.

2. Pour the mixture into a tall glass and serve immediately.

NUTRITIONAL FACTS PER SERVING

Calories: 170   Protein: 7 g   Carbohydrates: 24 g
Calcium: 147 mg   Total Fat: 2 g (11% fat cals)   Saturated Fat: 0.3 g

EXCHANGES, PER SERVING: 1 Lean Meat; 1½ Starch.

Chocolate Egg Cream

Yield: 1 serving
Prep. time: 5 minutes

3 tablespoons nondairy chocolate syrup

¼ cup reduced-fat soymilk

8 ounces seltzer water or club soda

A well-loved New York drink that probably never contained an egg!

1. Pour the chocolate syrup into a tall glass. Add the soymilk but do not stir. Add the seltzer water or club soda, and stir.

2. Serve immediately.

NUTRITIONAL FACTS PER SERVING

Calories: 160   Protein: 3.8 g   Carbohydrates: 31 g
Calcium: 150 mg   Total Fat: 1.6 g (9% fat cals)   Saturated Fat: 0 g

EXCHANGES, PER SERVING: 2 Starch.

Selected Bibliography

The following references offer the interested reader additional information about lactose sensitivity. These sources present material ranging from information on the ailment itself to listings of manufacturers of lactose-free products.

American Dietetic Association. *Food Sensitivity*. Chicago, IL: American Dietetic Association, 1985.

American Dietetic Association. *Handbook of Clinical Dietetics*. Chicago, IL: American Dietetic Association, 1992.

American Dietetic Association. *Lactose Intolerance*. The Food Sensitivity Series. Chicago, IL: American Dietetic Association, 1985.

Bayless, T., J. Rosenberg, and W. Walker. "When You Suspect Lactose Intolerance." *Patient Care*, 15 July 1980, 2.

Leary, W. "Just How Distressing Is Lactose Intolerance?" *The New York Times*, 12 July 1995.

Martens, R., and S. Martens. *The Milk Sugar Dilemma: Living With Lactose Intolerance*. East Lansing, MI: Medi-Ed Press, 1987.

Mirsky, P. *Lactose-Free Foods: A Shopper's Guide*. Wellesley, MA: Bullseye Information Services, 1994.

National Dairy Council. "Lactose Intolerance: Translating Research Information." *Summary of NDC Nutrition Research Conference*. July 1987.

"Nutritional Implications of Lactose and Lactose Activity." *Dairy Council Digest* 56 (1985): 5.

Tufts University. *Diet and Nutrition Letter* 12 (December 1994): 4.

Tufts University. *Diet and Nutrition Letter* (September 1995): 7.

Index